The Pursuit of the Presence

The Presence Series Volume 3

John Hammer

Copyright © 2025 by John Hammer

All rights reserved.

No part of this book may be reproduced in any form or by any electronic or mechanical means, including information storage and retrieval systems, without written permission from the author, except for the use of brief quotations in a book review.

All Scripture quotations, unless otherwise indicated, are taken from the Holy Bible, New International Version®, NIV®. Copyright ©1973, 1978, 1984, 2011 by Biblica, Inc.™ Used by permission of Zondervan. All rights reserved worldwide. www.zondervan.com The "NIV" and "New International Version" are trademarks registered in the United States Patent and Trademark Office by Biblica, Inc.™

Scriptures marked NKJV is taken from the New King James Version®. Copyright © 1982 by Thomas Nelson. Used by permission. All rights reserved.

Scripture marked KJV are taken from the Holy Bible, King James Version. Public Domain.

Contents

Praise for the Presence Series	vii
Acknowledgments	xi
Foreword	xv
Introduction	xvii
1. Generous Outpouring	1
2. Kiss the Son	3
3. The Lifter of My Head	5
4. Let Your Face Shine	7
5. Presence Denied	9
6. My Refuge	11
7. Fullness of Joy	13
8. Satisfied to See	15
9. Hind's Feet	17
10. Meditation	19
11. Who May Ascend?	21
12. Relief in Anguish	25
13. Love the House	27
14. One Thing	29
15. You are Surrounded	31
16. Presence Soundtrack	33
17. My Defender	35
18. Wait Patiently	37
19. As the Deer	39
20. Humbled Us	41
21. Love/Hate	45
22. Stillness in Trouble	49
23. Awaken the Dawn	53
24. The Higher Rock	55
25. Pour Out Your Heart	57
26. Thirsty	59
27. The Blessing of Nearness	61

28. Shout!	63
29. Shine On Us	65
30. Better is One Day	67
31. Hide Your Face?	69
32. The Secret Place	71
33. How We Come	75
34. The New Song and the Beauty of Holiness	77
35. Seek Him with All Your Heart	79
36. The Magnified	83
37. Presence Warfare	85
38. Everything Praise	89
39. Who May Dwell?	91
40. To and Fro	93
41. Diligently Seek	95
42. The Radiance of God's Glory	97
43. The Alive and Active Word	101
44. Approach with Confidence	103
45. A Better Offering	107
46. Walked with God	109
47. Off the Map	113
48. Seeing the Invisible	117
49. Ancient Future Faith	121
50. The Author and Finisher	123
51. Legitimate Sons	125
52. Without Holiness	127
53. Consuming Fire	131
54. The Highway of Holiness	135
55. Those Who Wait	139
56. The Awakened Ear	141
57. While He May Be Found	145
58. The Chosen Fast	149
59. Arise and Shine	153
60. Two Sins	155
61. Wholeheartedness	157
62. Wasted Dwelling	159
63. It is Good to Wait	163
64. Fire and Glory	165

65. Recapture	167
66. Dry Bones Live	169
67. Another in the Fire	173
68. Presence Price	177
69. The People Who Know	181
70. Altars Over Thrones	185
71. Double Portion	189
72. Rend Your Heart	193
73. Outpouring of Restoration Rain	197
74. Flow	199
75. Glory Covers	201
76. Moses's Tabernacle	203
77. The Offering	205
78. The Ark of The covenant	209
79. Inside the Ark	213
80. The Mercy Seat	215
81. The Table	219
82. The Lampstand	223
83. The Veil	225
84. The Altar	229
85. The Sacrifice	231
86. Deeper	235
87. Atonement Day	239
88. The Burning Lamp	243
89. The PreistHood	247
90. Consecration	251
91. Incense	255
92. Wash	257
Bibliography	261
Books by John Hammer	263
Contact	265
About the Author	267

Praise for the Presence Series

John Hammer's book is a masterful blend of theology, practical wisdom, personal stories, and lived experience. It not only inspires but challenges us to deepen our devotional lives in a way that feels accessible and transformative. This is a must-read for anyone looking to enrich their spiritual journey—I highly recommend it!

Dr. Joseph Mattera
Overseeing Bishop of *Christ to Covenant Coalition*

Love and tremendously appreciate the powerful and unique combination of a great intellect and beautiful heart that Pastor John possesses as a rising kingdom generational leader. This awesome book gives us wonderful insights surrounded by deep, biblically accurate theology. The outcome of reading this will be an increased hunger and deeper understanding of the presence of God.

Dr. Michael Maiden,
Lead pastor *Church for the Nations*, Phoenix, AZ.

John Hammer has written a fantastic series of devotional books that are sure to draw every reader into thoughtful worship, deep conviction, and a faith filled response to God's Word. As I read through each day, I found myself not only encouraged but looking forward to the next topic to ponder. These books are filled with Biblical truth, practical insights, and personal prayers that will help you to walk more closely with the Lord in your everyday life. I wholeheartedly recommend this series of books with great anticipation for how the Lord will use it in your life!

Pastor Ben Dixon
Lead Pastor - *Northwest Church*
Author - *Hearing God and Prophesy*

The Presence 4-part series written by John Hammer does an incredible job at inviting us as followers to not just know about God, but to live a life that is intimate with Him. *The Presence* captures the essence, attributes and beautiful mysteries of Christ, causing us to reflect and embrace our Savior from new depths and perspectives. John sets before us an insightful and thoughtful collection of writings that beg us to stop being busy for Jesus, but to actually know Him and walk with Him daily. In the current state of our world, we can't think of anything more important.

Sean & Christa Smith
Sean & Christa Smith Ministries

My son, John Hammer, has written a devotional on *The Presence* (of the Lord). My wife, Terry, and I used it for our daily devotions for a year. It was such a blessing to our daily walk with the Lord. The devotional was biblical, challenging, refreshing and, most importantly, brought us into His presence. Absorb yourself in it and you will be absorbed in His presence. Remember, Psalm 16 tells us "in His presence is fullness of joy!" Enjoy and enter His Presence as you read!

Dr. Dan C. Hammer
Sonrise Christian Center
Senior Apostolic Leader
Seattle Bible School President

This series of books exploring the presence of God, flows from John's heart of love for Jesus. John is a practical teacher with an ability to provoke you to desire Jesus in a deeper and more personal way. I have known John and his wife Grace for decades and have always been inspired by their simple love for Jesus, and their longing to serve Him well. In this season, we are ready to experience more of His presence and power in our lives every day. Let these books teach you how to open the eyes of your heart, and then engage in your walk with Jesus with greater joy, revelation, and authenticity.

Rachel Hickson
Heartcry for Change, Oxford, UK

Pastor John Hammer paints a picture of the beauty of Christ through both inspirational stories and theological truths. The Presence book feels similar to the strength and comfort found in an old friend who carries sound wisdom and holds your arms up when you're weary. It will lift your soul and draw you into the deep places of the Lord's heart! The Presence book is written in a way that will inspire you to hunger for more of Jesus each and every day.

Theo Koulianos Jr
A Place for Family

I have had the privilege of knowing John Hammer for nearly two decades, and I have always been inspired by his profound relationship with the Father. In every conversation, you sense that John is not just a man of knowledge and information, but someone with genuine experience and deep intimacy with the Lord. His writings on the presence of God are a reflection of this life of devotion. They are not mere teachings, but the fruit of years of inheritance and personal practice.
What I love about this book is its accessibility: it is easy to understand and follow for a new believer, yet it offers depth and wisdom for even the most seasoned and mature Christians. I wholeheartedly endorse and recommend this work to anyone seeking to grow in relationship with Jesus and deepen their revelation of Him."

Meesh Fomenko
Evangelist
Be Moved

A Christian cannot pursue Christ and not be in His Presence. His presence is the sustenance needed for a long-lasting Christian life. It is the pursuit of Him and His Word that draws on the presence of God.
In *The Presence*, John Hammer takes readers on a transformative journey into the heart of God's presence. Through vivid storytelling, profound biblical insights, and heartfelt prayers, each devotional invites you to experience the tangible nearness of God in everyday life. With every page, John masterfully intertwines Scripture and personal testimony, making the deep truths of God's love and mercy accessible and practical. This book is a treasure for anyone longing to encounter God more intimately and live with a renewed sense of awe and wonder. A must-read for seekers of His presence.

Paul Martini
Pastor of *New Life City*

Acknowledgments

First of all to all my daily blog readers and those of you who constantly commented and sent notes of encouragement along the journey of daily writing. What a joy you brought to me through your testimonies and personal insights you had along the way. I will always cherish that year of writing and the way it connected me with all of you.

A book can't come together without a great editor, thank you Carolyn for handling the edits but also the layout and process. This book series would have just stayed on the internet as blog posts if it wasn't for your effort and excellence turning it into a book. Thank you!

Mike Lewis, I am grateful for your design and art skills to produce such beautiful art. You brought our vision for arts and exalting Christ together for our church at Sonrise and I am very blessed to get to use some of the other works you produced for this cover art.

Jason, you are a man of many talents. Thank you for your work on the cover design. I appreciate your skillful work and heart to serve.

Jake, your idea to write this as a daily blog sparked something in me that helped bring all of this together. I'm so grateful for you sharing that with me.

Sonrise Christian Center, Elders, staff and members, thank you for being a church that goes after God's presence with all your heart. The past two years have been so incredible as God's manifest presence invades our gatherings. Your prayers, encouragement and support to write has been so wonderfully encouraging.

My family has been my biggest encouragement. My wife, and kids, Hailey, Emma, Justus and Addi all gave me the time to write. My dad and mom read my blog every day and encouraged me all along to make this a book. I'm so thankful for you all.

I'm most thankful for Jesus. Thank you for saving me and sharing Your presence with me. Thank You for carrying me through the darkest moments of my life and revealing Your nearness when I needed You the most.

I dedicate this book to my wife and best friend of 20 years, Grace Elaine. Your love for Jesus, prayers and constant encouragement to me made this work possible. I love you so much!

Foreword

"Come and see," Jesus invited in John 1:39. Eager to start a new life with purpose, John and Andrew are introduced to Jesus by John the Baptist. As they approach, Jesus turns and asks, "What do you want?" They respond by asking Him, "Where do you live? What is home to you?" Jesus replies, "Come and see." This invitation extends to us each day—to be with Jesus, follow Him, become like Him, and learn to live and love as He did.

After years of a busy schedule, I recently graduated with a doctorate. During a season of fatigue, the Holy Spirit whispered, "Leif, hurry is one of love's greatest enemies." It's challenging to be fully present with His presence when we're constantly in a rush. The next invitation was clear: to slow down enough to catch up with God (1 John 4:16 reminds us, "God is love").

Our Heavenly Father calls us to a major upgrade in the quality and depth of our life and ministry. As I daily practice His presence, I was asked to write the foreword for this devotional about experiencing the presence of God. I first met John Hammer in 2004 when Dr. Randy Clark invited me to teach at the first healing school in Seattle. John and I instantly connected as family and friends. Today, Pastor John and his wife, Grace, lead a Kingdom-focused church and movement that transforms lives, impacts regions, and disciples nations. It has been my honor to serve as one of John's spiritual fathers, observing his deep commitment to hosting the presence of Jesus. His journey in sonship and leadership serves as an example of what it means to walk with the Father and love others, defining the promised land God calls us to occupy. John's passionate, infectious love for the Lord has always inspired me.

John carries a "love virus" that can only be caught in the secret place, where he learns to host God's presence. I have seen him live this message, even as he walked through the valley of the shadow of death. Through difficult seasons, I witnessed Jesus preparing a table for him in the presence of his enemies. In all circumstances, John found sustenance in God's presence, making it a daily practice that leads to wholeness and holiness. John, your guide on this journey, is raw, real, relational, relevant, radical, and a revivalist.

The daily bread John serves is rich with power, love, and wisdom. I challenge both you and myself to invest 15 minutes each day in encountering God—to know Him, experience Him, and meet Him face to face. May we experience His nearness, His heart, His nature, and His ways, allowing love to become the mark of our true maturity. After encountering Him, we then encounter who we are—our identity, potential, values, desires, gifts, and limitations. These all begin to reflect the image of the One we behold, and He is the One we are becoming and will release to the world.

May your heart be hungry and your mind open as John, like a master chef, prepares daily meals at the table of God's presence. The best of who you are will only be discovered in His presence. Jesus will be your host, inviting you to His table where the cup of life overflows. John will serve you the daily bread, freshly prepared by Jesus. Come and see, and come and taste.

Dr. Leif Hetland
   President of *Global Mission Awareness*
   Author of *The Love Awakening*

Introduction

The Presence started as a book idea about the power of thankfulness several years ago and has now turned into a 4-volume series as a 365-day devotional. I wrote The Presence as a daily blog/newsletter originally on my Substack platform after struggling with how to bring this book together. My heart and vision was to inspire people to live daily in the presence of God through thanksgiving, worship, and wonder.

Every time I tried to write on the power of thanksgiving, I would only come up with more ideas and I couldn't pull a book together. I was so inspired whenever I wrote on this subject, but I couldn't bring my thoughts on the topic together in a unified way until I realized one day that The Presence would really work so much better as a daily devotional filled with short thoughts to help people draw near to God.

My friend Jake once told me about a book writing idea where you could write each chapter as a blog and let people comment and interact with your work while you were writing. To be honest, I didn't like the idea for my own personal style when I heard him share that with me. But when I realized I had a daily devotional to write, the idea returned to me and motivated me to put it to work.

I talked things over with Grace and said I really want to write this book as a daily blog, but I need to know how you feel about it. And as my biggest encouragement, she cheered me on and said go for it.

When I first started writing, I wasn't sure if this would be 30, 60 or 90 days; or if I could make it a full 365. So, I started writing usually in the evening and scheduling each daily post at 4am the next morning. A few days I forgot to write and scrambled to catch up. Some days felt like heaven on earth, where I was bursting with wonder and excitement. Other days felt completely cold emotionally. It felt like a grind at times but by the time I reached 90 days I thought that I could maybe do the whole year.

By the grace of God and my wife, I made it the whole year, of course. As we started the publishing process, it became apparent that this book could end up being over 1,000 pages, so my editor approached me with the idea of doing a multi-part series. Hence, *The Presence Series* was born.

The 4-part volumes are titled: *The Lord of the Presence, The Power of the Presence, The Pursuit of the Presence and The Wonder of the Presence*.

The Lord of the Presence covers January through March. This first volume starts with an overview of the major themes of this whole book series. From there, the rest of volume one is devoted to God's character and nature through His names, His attributes and the nature of God the Father and God the Son.

The Power of the Presence covers April through June. This second volume continues on Jesus, the Son of God, the Holy Spirit and Paul's writings on the Presence of God.

The Pursuit of the Presence covers July through September. This third volume comes from the Psalms, the Prophets and the tabernacle of Moses.

The Wonder of the Presence covers October through December. This fourth and final volume begins with more on the tabernacles, the temples and the corporate presence of God throughout the Scriptures. It is wrapped up with a collection of thoughts on wonder and thanksgiving that lead up to the Incarnation throughout December. And finally, everything comes together as we focus on the return of Jesus, where all the saints will be with God forever in His manifest presence.

Each day begins with a Scripture reading and usually some kind of personal story or illustration from life. Then each daily devotional ends with a prayer. This work is Christ-centered, Trinitarian, simple and yet filled with theology. It's charismatic and promotes a Spirit-filled life of devotion.

I still don't feel qualified to share a work like this because I still need to grow in my own devotion in spending time alone in God's presence. Even in this season of publishing, I have been repenting of time wasters and distractions that I have let disrupt my time alone with Jesus. I offer this book not as an expert but as a fellow sojourner who is learning to frame success in life by being with Jesus and becoming more like Him.

I offer you this work with humility. Thank you for taking it up. May God use this work to grow your longing for the only One who can fulfill the longing of your soul, and may He be exalted in your life as you read and apply this work to your life.

Generous Outpouring
July 1

But when the kindness and love of God our Savior appeared, he saved us, not because of righteous things we had done, but because of his mercy. He saved us through the washing of rebirth and renewal by the Holy Spirit, whom he poured out on us generously through Jesus Christ our Savior, so that, having been justified by his grace, we might become heirs having the hope of eternal life.
Titus 3:4-7

Have you ever had a refillable drink?

I remember when I was young, almost no restaurants had refillable drinks. I remember how my mind was blown when I was a kid, and they told me I could have free refills.

This generous outpouring amazed me as they brought me beverage after beverage. Now almost all restaurants have refillable coffee, tea or soda. If I go to eat at a place and they charge for each drink, I can hardly believe it.

In Christ, we experience a generous outpouring of the Holy Spirit.

As we covered earlier in this series, we can describe the Holy Spirt as God's empowering Presence in our lives.

In Christ, we have received the generous outpouring of God's empowering Presence.

God's kindness and love as our Savior has appeared. He has saved us. This is not by our righteous works, but by His mercy.

Jesus saved us by the washing and renewal of the Holy Spirit, who He poured out on us.

The Holy Spirit is poured on us generously.

The Holy Spirit is poured out over and over.

There are continual refills available.

His outpouring brings us an abundance. He is generous with giving us Himself!

We live with a lack of God's Presence by our own decision. God has been generous to pour out the Presence and He doesn't hold back.

How much of God do you want?

We have everything we need because it is by grace that we are justified, and become heirs who have the hope of eternal life.

We are in with Him by grace.

It is done and paid for.

But are we living in the generous overflow of His Presence?

Its's time to receive all He has for us as He gives of Himself so generously.

God, my Savior, You have been kind, and You have loved me. You saved me not because of what I have done, but by Your mercy. You saved me through the washing of rebirth and renewal by the Holy Spirit. You have poured out Your Spirit, Your empowering Presence, over my life with so much generosity. I want more of You. Thank you for Your grace. I receive of Your generosity. In Jesus' name, amen.

Kiss the Son
July 2

Serve the Lord with fear and celebrate his rule with trembling. Kiss his son, or he will be angry and your way will lead to your destruction, for his wrath can flare up in a moment. Blessed are all who take refuge in him.
Psalms 2:11-12

How near do you have to be someone to kiss them?

Is there a more vulnerable place than being in a position to give or receive a kiss? Kisses can be romantic, but they may also be affection shown to your child, or honor to a friend or family member.

The one thing about a kiss is that no matter if it's to a spouse, or a cultural greeting to a neighbor, you have to be close to share one. You have to be in the presence of someone to share this exchange of warmth or respect.

In Psalm 2, the kings and nations of the earth are plotting against God the Father and against His Son, the Messiah, who we know is Jesus. The Lord hears the plans of these conspirators who long to take rulership of the earth away from Him and He laughs at them. As the Psalm comes to a close, we are called to "serve the Lord with fear and celebrate His rule with trembling."

Then the Psalmist says to "Kiss His Son."

How do we escape the evil of world rulers and the corruption that is in the nations? We give our devotion and affection to Jesus. We get close enough to kiss the Son.

God's wrath and judgement will bring destruction on the earth, but all of us who have taken refuge in Jesus will be blessed and saved.

The key for us during times of political unrest and chaos in the nation is to exalt Jesus the Son of God and take refuge in Him.

We don't need to be afraid. God has a plan to give the nations to Jesus as an inheritance. Evil will not triumph over God's righteous Son.

The evil see God as tyrant but the righteous see God as a refuge.

When Jesus becomes beautiful to us, we draw close to give Him our love. The Lord becomes our refuge, and we are protected in the Presence.

There is a place of safety for us in uncertain times.

"Blessed are all who take refuge in Him."

King Jesus, Son of God, I take refuge in You. I draw near to kiss You. I count You as precious above all. I have chosen to serve You with fear and celebrate Your rule with trembling. You are my hiding place. You are my place of safety and refuge. I do not need to worry about the plans of evildoers, for You are exalted as the Ruler of all. In Your good and mighty name, amen.

The Lifter of My Head
July 3

But you, Lord, are a shield around me, my glory, the One who lifts my head high. I call out to the Lord, and he answers me from his holy mountain.
Psalms 3:3-4

What do you do to overcome discouragement?

When I am discouraged, the most encouraging thing for me is prayer and worship, especially when I do it in a beautiful space with a view of the water.

The other thing I do is talk with my wife, my dad, or one of my close friends. A good conversation with God or someone else I can be transparent with can give me strength to face whatever is going in my life.

We all need someone to lift us up from time to time.

In Psalm 3, David is king when he writes this and his son Absalom has turned against him. Absalom is trying to have David killed and has turned thousands of people against him as well. David is literally on the run for his life at this point.

Most of us won't face this dire of circumstances, but we will face betrayal, disloyalty, people being angry with us, and people who have it out for us.

David loved his son so much, and it was heartbreaking to have him plot against him. The greater love we have for someone, when it is not reciprocated, the greater it can hurt.

But David had a source of strength even in such a heart wrenching situation, he knew the Lord was his shield.

He called the Lord, "my glory, the One who lifts my head high."

When our greatest glory is the Lord, everything else can be falling apart in life, but we can stay encouraged. This doesn't mean that everything in life is easy, but who is your greatest source of glory?

Do you glory in your accomplishments?

Do you glory in success?

Do you glory in relationships?

Do you glory in other's opinions of you?

The key to staying encouraged is to glory in the Lord God.

When we call to Him, He answers us.

Oh, what a friend we have in Him.

He is so faithful to always be there to lift us up.

With Him, we always have the gift of a prayer. He is there to shield us and listen to us.

When you are down, glory in the Lord and He will lift your head.

Lord God, I love You! When others betray me and come after me to attack me in life, I can run to You. You are my shield. You are my glory and the lifter of my head. Lift me up. Fill my heart with courage as I take refuge in You. When I call to You, You answer me. You are faithful. In Jesus' name, amen.

Let Your Face Shine
July 4

Many, Lord, are asking, "Who will bring us prosperity?" Let the light of your face shine on us. Fill my heart with joy when their grain and new wine abound. In peace I will lie down and sleep, for you alone, Lord, make me dwell in safety.
Psalms 4:6-8

What do you do when you are under stress?

Are you a stress shopper or a stress eater?

Of course, those are bad ways to deal with stress, but do you have any good ways to deal with stress?

When I am under stress, it helps me to get in a quiet place with God. I like to read or do some sort of physical sport. I like to laugh and do something fun.

It also really helps to spend time with God. Being in His Presence makes the difference in my life.

Sometimes my wife says, "Do you need some alone time with God?"

And when she says that she is right.

David is under pressure and stress in Psalm 4. He is under the pressure of leadership and dealing with great challenges. His heart's cry is for the light of God's face to shine upon Him and the people of His kingdom. He confesses he will lie down in peace and sleep, for the Lord will make Him dwell in safety.

David starts Psalm 4 in prayer because he is under great duress, but he ends the prayer in peace and rest.

The difference is knowing the power of the Presence.

What is the Presence?

Again, it is being close to God.

When we are in the presence of someone, we are before them. We are with them and near them. There is nothing more Presence driven then "Let the light of your face shine on us."

What brings us into peace?

When God allows His face to shine upon us.

What releases us from our stress?

When God allows His face to shine upon us.

What grants us success where others are pressuring us?

When God allows His face to shine upon us.

What causes us to make it through something we feel we could fail at?

When God allows His face to shine upon us.

The Presence of His face shining upon us gives us favor and rest. True peace comes when God turns toward us and smiles upon us. God not only answers our prayers, He gives us Himself, His Presence, and we are renewed in that place of meeting with Him.

Lord, You hear my cry for help. Deliver me from the stress and pressures of life. Be magnified in my life. Let the light of Your face shine on me. Allow me to be at peace and rest. You cause me to dwell in safety. You are my favorite dwelling place. Come close Lord, I want to behold Your face. Show me who You are. In Jesus' name, amen.

Presence Denied
July 5

The arrogant cannot stand in your presence. You hate all who do wrong.
Psalms 5:5

Why do you think we don't like it when someone is proud? I think it can often be that we don't like pride in someone else because it reminds us of our own pride.

There are a lot of warnings in the Bible against pride.

Pride is what made Lucifer the devil.

Pride robs us of God's best.

We were created for God, and pride and arrogance cause us to attempt to live independently of Him.

The one thing that will deny us the Presence is to live in pride and arrogance. What a costly thing pride is. We thrive in the Presence of God.

Jesus paid for us to be able to stand in God's Presence.

David was a forerunner who experienced God's Presence by faith. He knew about the importance of our heart posture before God.

In Psalm 5, there is a contrast between the prideful and the evildoers and David, who bows before the Lord. Those who are humble and make God their refuge or dwelling place, are surrounded by God.

But let all who take refuge in you be glad; let them ever sing for joy. Spread your protection over them, that those who love your name may rejoice in you. Surely, Lord, you bless the righteous; you surround them with your favor as with a shield (Psalms 5:11-12).

When you live in pride, you are denied, when you live in surrender, you are surrounded by favor.

Pride makes you vulnerable and lacking God's Presence, where being humble before God puts you in a place of favor. The favor of God becomes a shield to those who live in worship and dependence upon the Lord.

Pride will cost you the Presence and the favor of God surrounding you. We can be surrounded by so many things that are disturbing and challenging in life.

Why sacrifice being surrounded by favor in the Presence of God?

Lord, I do not want to be denied access into Your Presence. I turn from arrogance and pride. I bow before You. I take refuge in You, and I am glad. I sing for joy. Spread Your protection over me. I love Your name! Surely, you bless me and surround me with Your favor as with a shield. This is the place I want to dwell, in Your Presence and surrounded by Your favor. In Jesus' name, amen.

My Refuge
July 6

Lord my God, I take refuge in you; save and deliver me from all who pursue me.
Psalms 7:1

Where do you run for refuge when things get tough?

As a pastor, I've heard people describe their vice or addiction as a place of safety.

As I've heard Leif Hetland say many times, "Pain seeks pleasure."

When we are in pain, we can turn to negative behaviors that give us pleasure.

When we are deceived by sin, we medicate our pain with things that cover our pain but don't heal us or offer us true protection.

When I've heard people longing to hold on to their bad habit or unhealthy relationship as if it is a refuge, they say something like, "But what would I turn to without this?"

The answer to what you turn to without that feel good thing in your life is JESUS! You turn to the Lord your God, who is the ultimate refuge and deliverer.

You need to see things that offer you pleasure but are ungodly as idols and false gods that cannot truly hold you, heal you, or protect you from what is really going on in life.

You make God your refuge by forsaking all other places of refuge. You make God your refuge by spending time with Him in prayer. You practice His Presence, and He shields and protects you. He ministers to the needs of your heart.

When He is your refuge, you are saved and delivered from all who pursue you.

David learned to sing these love songs to the Lord, and the Lord gave David protection and deliverance from evil. You might not be seeking the same type of help that David needed, but these songs David wrote were written in deep times of need.

No matter how deep your need is, you can run to Jesus as your refuge. You can experience the Presence as you sing to the Lord and turn your affections towards Him.

Bill Johnson has often advised when you are facing discouragement or trials to read the Psalms until you find your own voice. You can find what you are going through in the Psalms, or something that sounds like what you are facing in your emotions.

Let these words and songs become your own prayers. Worship God and take refuge in Him.

Lord my God, You are my refuge. You are my hiding place. I forsake all lesser loves and refuges that give me false comfort. You save me and deliver me. I bring You songs and prayers to touch Your heart. There is no one like You. I love You! In Jesus' name, amen.

Fullness of Joy
July 7

You make known to me the path of life; you will fill me with joy in your presence, with eternal pleasures at your right hand.
Psalms 16:11

Who brings you the most joy?

My wife brings me the most joy. To be in her presence often means a good laugh and a fun time. I have described her as a self-contained party. Of course, she goes through hard times and challenges like anyone else, but she has always been the most joyful person I have ever known. She smiles so much sometimes she gets a sore face. Just being with her has taught me so much about joy and enjoying this life God has given us.

In Psalm 16, David makes a connection with joy and God's Presence. It's no wonder that my wife can access God's Presence so easily since she is so joyful. David said that we are filled with joy in God's Presence or, as some translations say, in God's Presence there is fullness of joy. He continues declaring that there are eternal pleasures at God's right hand. In the Presence there is full joy and eternal pleasure.

God not only wants us to know about Him, but to know Him and enjoy Him. I love what the Westminster catechism says, "Man's chief end is to know God and enjoy Him forever." *

People of the Presence have an unlimited and eternal source of joy. The Lord Himself is full of joy and being in His Presence causes us to become like Him.

We don't often tend to use the word "pleasure" as a word that we associate with God. But there is pleasure in the Presence of God.

We often settle so easily for worldly pleasure and often associate it with things that are negative. But God loves to give us pleasure.

Knowing God should be our greatest delight. His Presence is our reward. The more you cultivate a life in the Presence, the more you enjoy being with Him. Jesus is our highest prize. There is nothing more enjoyable than knowing Him and being in His Presence. His Presence eases our burdens, lightens our hearts and causes us to rejoice.

There is no one like our God.

———

Lord God, I love You so much! I delight in You. I love Your Presence. Your Presence brings me fullness of joy and there is pleasure in loving You. I have set my love upon You, and I love getting to know You more. Let me not be satisfied with inferior pleasure. Let my greatest joy and delight be found in You. In Jesus' name, amen.

SATISFIED TO SEE
JULY 8

As for me, I will be vindicated and will see your face; when I awake, I will be satisfied with seeing your likeness.
Psalms 17:15

If you are married, was there a more exciting moment in life than seeing your spouse for the first time on your wedding day?

The moment I saw my wife Grace on our wedding day will be forever etched in my memory.

It was one of the greatest moments of my life.

I know that traditionally the groom does not see the bride until she is presented by her father in the ceremony and unveiled. However, with pictures and everything nowadays, the revealing of the bride can be a special moment as part of the pre-wedding activities.

I had my back turned to her and they brought her in to meet me. The photographer, family and wedding party were looking on and then I was told to turn around. Wow! What a moment! I got to behold the one my soul loves in her beauty and splendor as we were about to commit to one another for a union in holy marriage.

King David was a man of the Presence. In Psalm 17, he lifts a beautiful prayer to the Lord. Part way through, he exclaims the intimacy and protection that comes from someone who prays and dwells in God's Presence: "I call on you, my God, for you will answer me; turn your ear to me and hear my prayer. Show me the wonders of your great love, you who save by your right hand those who take refuge in you from their foes. Keep me as the apple of your eye; hide me in the shadow of your wings (Psalms 17:6-8 NIV)."

David knew that protection flowed from being a man of prayer who deeply loved God and His Presence about all else.

As the Psalm continues, David says that the true vindication he will receive is when he will see the face of the Lord. What if we believed that the greatest vindication we could receive for our troubles was to see God's face? This is Presence soaked language. This is a man who is a lover of God. The cry of those of the Presence is "Show me Your face, Lord."

David continued that when he was awake, he would be satisfied with seeing God's likeness. Seeing God is what satisfies.

In the Presence we behold the Lord, and in seeing Him, our soul is satisfied. Our greatest vindication is not always success as the world counts it or everything going our way, it is seeing the One our soul loves.

When we call on Him, He answers us. He shows us the wonder of His love. He saves us and is our refuge. He keeps us as the apple of His eyes and hides us in the shadow of His wings.

O, that He would be our refuge, our hiding place. May we see Him and be satisfied.

Lord, You satisfy me. I want to see You. I want to behold You as I dwell in Your Presence. Hide me in Your Presence. Hide me under Your wings. You are my refuge. Let me see Your face. Let my soul be satisfied in seeing Your likeness. In Jesus' name, amen.

Hind's Feet
July 9

As for God, his way is perfect: The word of the LORD is tried: He is a buckler to all those that trust in him. For who is God save the LORD? Or who is a rock save our God? It is God that girdeth me with strength, And maketh my way perfect. He maketh my feet like hinds' feet, And setteth me upon my high places.
Psalm 18:30-33 KJV

Do you enjoy watching the movements of a deer?

In the home we currently live in, we occasionally get visits from deer. They are such beautiful creatures. I love to see the way they run. In the King James version of Psalm 18, David talks about how God makes his feet like a hind, or a female deer. While a female deer, a hind, is running, they are able to place their back feet directly in the same spot as their front feet to more effectively lose a predator that pursues them.

Psalm 18 is about God delivering David from his enemies and from Saul. It is a beautiful Psalm to sing and pray in its entirety. David says in verse 30 that God's way is perfect.

As my dad's friend used to say, "It's pretty hard to improve on perfection."

God's Word has been tried. It is perfect not only in theory but in practice and trial. His Word is trustworthy, and He becomes our buckler or shield.

The Presence is the place where God shields those who trust in Him. He is our Savior and our Rock.

This is Messianic language because these descriptions of the Lord ultimately end up being fulfilled in Jesus. We can base our life on Him and in His Presence, we are protected and saved. He gives us strength and calls us to the high places as we escape our enemies.

God wants to give us experiences in the heights of His glory, but He does it through helping shield us as He leads us to escape our enemies. It is often through the challenges and problems of life that we learn to ascend to the high places God has for us. His Presence is our reward, and He calls us higher to be with Him.

The Lord delights in empowering us like the deer to escape and walk on the high places. Though the journey might be difficult and dangerous, you can make it. How different would things be if we could see things from His perspective and keep a perfect trust in Him?

He is perfect, and He is there for us. He is faithful to defend us and call us to ascend into the heights of His loving Presence.

Lord, who is like You? You are my Savior, my Rock, my Shield and You are my Reward. I trust in You. You have made my feet like the deer that escapes her enemies. You call me to the high places. I long to ascend with You even through the challenges. Though the journey may be difficult, I will rely upon Your Presence, and I will make it as the deer. In Jesus' name, amen.

MEDITATION
JULY 10

May these words of my mouth and this meditation of my heart be pleasing in your sight, Lord, my Rock and my Redeemer.
Psalms 19:14

Have you ever spent time in meditation?
Just the idea of meditation within Christian circles seems to be underappreciated. Meditation is much more en vogue within new age and eastern religious circles these days.

But meditation is a very Christian idea and very important for those who practice the Presence

New age and eastern religious meditation has to do with the emptying of oneself. But Christian meditation has to do with fullness and completeness. The Christian who meditates is full of the Holy Spirit and fills their mind by focusing on the Word of God and the nature of who God is.

David's prayer in Psalm 19 is so beautiful and it culminates with this request that the words of his mouth and the mediation of his heart would be pleasing in the sight of the Lord. David knows the Lord is listening to the words of our mouth and the meditation of our hearts. God is present with us. When we spend time meditating on God's Word and God's nature, we become aware of His Presence.

Meditation is about giving ourselves fully to one focus that we might be fully consumed with God.

To meditate, you must remove distractions and get to a quiet place. In meditation, you start to focus and pray on one Scripture seeking to extract every morsel of spiritual nutrient from it.

Or you may focus on one aspect of God's character and nature. As you do this and you pray and think upon our precious Lord, you will become more aware of how near He is.

In our busy lives, we may read Scripture, listen to Scripture or even memorize Scripture. But the greatest power is when we begin to meditate on the Scriptures. Our mind and our affections are shaped by who God is and His holy Word.

Pray and sing the Scriptures. Repeat them over and over. And give your mind to God fully. May His perfect Word form your desires and be the meditation of your heart.

Lord God, teach me to meditate on who You are and upon Your holy Word. Fill me up. Fill my mind with Your thoughts. I want to please and touch Your heart with my words and meditation. You are my Rock and my Redeemer. There is no one like You. Shape me and mold me in Your Presence as I fix my mind upon You. In Jesus' name, amen.

Who May Ascend?
July 11

Who may ascend the mountain of the Lord? Who may stand in his holy place? The one who has clean hands and a pure heart, who does not trust in an idol or swear by a false god. They will receive blessing from the Lord and vindication from God their Savior. Such is the generation of those who seek him, who seek your face, God of Jacob. Lift up your heads, you gates; be lifted up, you ancient doors, that the King of glory may come in. Who is this King of glory? The Lord strong and mighty, the Lord mighty in battle. Lift up your heads, you gates; lift them up, you ancient doors, that the King of glory may come in. Who is he, this King of glory? The Lord Almighty— he is the King of glory.
Psalms 24:3-10

Have you ever climbed a mountain or gone on a hike?

One of the things I never really did very much before I got married to Grace was go on hikes.

In the Pacific Northwest we have dozens and dozens, if not hundreds, of breathtaking hikes. We are surrounded by mountains, forests, rivers, lakes and streams. Hiking to mountain tops in our region in the summer gives one views of how we live in one of the most beautiful areas in the world.

One thing about a hike is that you don't go casually, you prepare your supplies; you determine your route and you prioritize your plans. If you want to ascend, you are making it a priority.

Psalm 24 is one of my favorite Psalms.

David says there is a requirement for the one who wants to hike up mount Zion. Zion is the holy hill, a sanctuary that will become the place of Jerusalem. It represents the Lord's Presence and the Lord's rule.

It is the place Jesus will return to one day.

David says here in verse three, "Who may ascend the hill of the Lord?"

The one who may approach the Presence here is one who has clean hands and a pure heart. One who has not trusted idols or sworn by false gods.

David says those who ascend, those who go up to be with the Lord, those who go to the Presence where the Lord dwells, these are the ones who seek God's face like Jacob.

Jacob didn't start out right, but he wrestled with the Lord and received the Lord's blessing. He held on until He was transformed.

We are those who seek God's face until He blesses us.

Then, David looks to this prophetic Messianic victory of the coming King. He begins to speak to the ancient doors and gates of authority and commands them to be opened so that the King of glory will come in.

Jesus is the King of glory.

Jesus is coming back to the hill or the mountain of the Lord. We who ascend His holy hill to be in His Presence are granted authority to speak to gates and doors to be opened in His name.

There is a measure we see now of the Presence of the King of glory, but there is a future literal Presence when He returns in His glorified body to triumph over His enemies and bring victory to His people.

May we ascend His holy hill to be with Him.

King of glory, come! King of glory, I welcome Your Presence. I want to ascend Your holy mountain and stand in Your holy place. Give me clean hands and a pure heart that I might seek Your face. Lord, strong and mighty, come in through the ancient doors. You are the Lord almighty. In Jesus' name, amen.

Relief in Anguish
July 12

Turn to me and be gracious to me, for I am lonely and afflicted. Relieve the troubles of my heart and free me from my anguish. Look on my affliction and my distress and take away all my sins. See how numerous are my enemies and how fiercely they hate me! Guard my life and rescue me; do not let me be put to shame, for I take refuge in you.
Psalms 25:16-20

Have you ever had an ugly cry?

Is there someone that you can cry with and know that they won't judge you but will help you?

I've had some good cries in my life. I've appreciated some of the work of Jason Wilson who wrote a book called *Cry like a Man*. He's a strong man and lifetime martial artist who trains young men through martial arts how to overcome obstacles in their character and succeed in life. When boys cry in his program, he affirms to them it's okay to cry as a man, and teaches them how to work through their emotions.

I'm thankful for my dad and the men in my life who have taught me to be both strong and express my emotions.

In Psalm 25, David shows us that the Presence is a place where we can be real with our emotions. David brings up his emotions of being lonely, afflicted, in anguish and distress. He is being pursued by his enemies and doesn't want to be put to shame.

David's hope in his anguish is being with the Lord. He uses that Presence language, "I take refuge in You."

I want you to see here in Psalm 25 that David is being vulnerable and honest with his emotions. He is pouring his heart out to God and sharing his feelings.

It's wrong and immature to live by your emotions, but it is also wrong and immature to stuff your emotions. David is honest with God about his anguish.

The Presence is a place of suffering. It's a place where you can suffer in the emotions of anguish and affliction. You can ugly cry when you are alone with God.

As you work through your emotions that hurt, you can form prayers like David, for God to be gracious to you and relieve the troubles of your heart.

God is not put off by our honesty and our hurts. He is put off when we are arrogant and prideful. He wants to be the place where we can run to when we are hurting and pour out our heart before Him.

He loves it when we call upon Him in our pain for Him to rescue us. He is always there for us as a refuge. His Presence is our relief in our anguish.

Lord, I look to You. I have felt alone and afflicted. I have been in anguish and distress. I've felt pursued by enemies, and I need You to save me. Be gracious to me and relieve the troubles of my heart. When I am hurting, I can take refuge in You. I come to you honestly in my pain and ask that You take away my sins. Protect me and save me. I run to You. In Jesus' name, amen.

Love the House
July 13

Lord, I love the house where you live, the place where your glory dwells.
Psalms 26:8

Did you have a favorite house to visit when you were growing up?

What made it your favorite?

I remember loving to go my aunt's house and to my family friend's house. There was something about being with my family and another family.

What made a house great were the people who lived in it. It was people's kindness and hospitality. But it was also the exchange of stories and laughter that ultimately was about sharing our lives.

King David had a favorite house to visit, the house of the Lord. David loved the house the Lord lived in because it was the place where God's glory dwelt. We were made to dwell with God. We were made for His house.

The desire for the Presence is as ancient as Eden. God established Eden as a dwelling place, a house for God. All through the Scriptures, the idea of God dwelling with His people in His house or temple unfolds from Genesis to Revelation. David loved to dwell with God.

As believers in Jesus after the cross, we become the house of God, the place His glory dwells.

Can you say with David, "I love the place where You live God?"

Dwelling with God creates a relationship history where you share life with Him. This is not only a fellowship you enjoy like you do with another person, this is a fellowship with the living God and Creator of all things.

His glory waits to be encountered and known by you. We love to be with God because His glory brings us joy as we connect with the eternal longing of our souls.

The Lord wants to share Himself with us and He desires fellowship where we share our life with Him.

David lived in this reality. David knew how to dwell with God in His house and experience God's glory. There is nothing like the weighty Presence of God.

There are many places we can choose to dwell. David is forsaking all the lesser places in Psalm 26 so he might dwell in the ultimate place, the place where God lives. That's where I want to live my life, the place where He dwells.

Lord, You are my dwelling place. I love the house where You live. You have made me Your house, but how easily I can become distracted or busy and miss the glory You want to share with me. I want to abide in the place where Your glory dwells. Keep me in that place of fellowship and the sharing of our lives. I love to be with You. In Jesus' name, amen.

One Thing
July 14

One thing I ask from the Lord, this only do I seek: that I may dwell in the house of the Lord all the days of my life, to gaze on the beauty of the Lord and to seek him in his temple.
Psalms 27:4

If you had one thing you could ask God for, what would it be?
That is a hard question for me to answer. Think about it. I mean, it can only be one thing.

David tells us in Psalm 27 what his one thing is all about.

His one thing is to only seek that He might dwell in the house of the Lord all the days of his life and gaze upon the beauty of the Lord. This is Presence language. In fact, maybe of all the Psalms, this is the greatest cry for the Presence.

David longs to be with God and gaze upon His beauty.
David loved God.
David was a man of the Presence.
David knew how to dwell and simply be with God.
The Psalms are worshipful and Presence soaked, but Psalm 27 seems

to capture more than anything the heart behind why I write this daily devotional.

I want to include the full Psalm in today's entry as the prayer. May God make the one thing that David asked Him for, the one thing that we ask Him for.

The Lord is my light and my salvation— whom shall I fear? The Lord is the stronghold of my life— of whom shall I be afraid? When the wicked advance against me to devour me, it is my enemies and my foes who will stumble and fall. Though an army besiege me, my heart will not fear; though war break out against me, even then I will be confident. One thing I ask from the Lord, this only do I seek: that I may dwell in the house of the Lord all the days of my life, to gaze on the beauty of the Lord and to seek him in his temple. For in the day of trouble he will keep me safe in his dwelling; he will hide me in the shelter of his sacred tent and set me high upon a rock. Then my head will be exalted above the enemies who surround me; at his sacred tent I will sacrifice with shouts of joy; I will sing and make music to the Lord. Hear my voice when I call, Lord; be merciful to me and answer me. My heart says of you, "Seek his face!" Your face, Lord, I will seek. Do not hide your face from me, do not turn your servant away in anger; you have been my helper. Do not reject me or forsake me, God my Savior. Though my father and mother forsake me, the Lord will receive me. Teach me your way, Lord; lead me in a straight path because of my oppressors. Do not turn me over to the desire of my foes, for false witnesses rise up against me, spouting malicious accusations. I remain confident of this: I will see the goodness of the Lord in the land of the living. Wait for the Lord; be strong and take heart and wait for the Lord (Psalm 27:1-14) In Jesus' name, amen.

You are Surrounded
July 15

You are my hiding place; you will protect me from trouble and surround me with songs of deliverance.
Psalms 32:7

Do you have a favorite sermon?

I grew up as a pastor's kid. I've heard my dad preach hundreds and hundreds of sermons.

I think my favorite sermon I've ever heard him preach was titled *Surrounded*. His tag line he repeats over and over in the sermon is, "You are surrounded, you will surrender."

He formed this sermon by mining the Scriptures on the topic of being surrounded by enemies, by angels and by God Himself.

It will be one that sticks with me forever.

The truth my dad laid out in that sermon is that we are often surrounded by many forces and realities in life, but we have to choose if we are going to surrender to God's surround, or the surround of the evil one.

David is often surrounded by trouble in life. He is surrounded by the discouragement of his own sin, by enemies trying to kill him, by his family relationships that are strained and by the people he leads pressing him to respond to difficult circumstances.

But here in Psalm 32, David is declaring that He is ultimately surrounded by the Lord.

People of the Presence face many difficulties and challenges in life, but like David, we know Who surrounds us. We know the Lord is our hiding place who protects us in trouble.

The Lord not only surrounds us, He surrounds us with songs of deliverance.

Think about that. God surrounds us with songs. God is our hiding place, and He sings over us. He sings over us songs of freedom and salvation. He is there for us in trouble to encourage us and lift us up.

How often do we waste our energy by focusing on the wrong things that surround us?

What if you started to focus on the Lord and confess that He is surrounding you in your trouble?

What if you remember that you are hidden in Him?

What if you ask the Lord to let you hear the songs He sings over you?

There is something about being surrounded by a song, the song that comes from the Lord that brings me comfort and lets me experience the Presence. This trouble you feel surrounded by might be an opportunity to run into the One who is your hiding place and hear His victory song.

You are surrounded, you will surrender.

Surrender to the One who loves you and delivers you.

Lord God, I run to You, my hiding place. You are my protector in trouble. You surround me. I surrender to You. I am safe with You. There is no One like You, my God. You sing over me. You sing songs of deliverance. Your song brings me into freedom. I love Your song over me. I love Your Presence. In Jesus' name, amen.

Presence Soundtrack
July 16

Sing joyfully to the Lord, you righteous; it is fitting for the upright to praise him. Praise the Lord with the harp; make music to him on the ten-stringed lyre. Sing to him a new song; play skillfully, and shout for joy. For the word of the Lord is right and true; he is faithful in all he does. The Lord loves righteousness and justice; the earth is full of his unfailing love.
Psalms 33:1-5

Do you like soundtracks?

I love movie soundtracks. Some days, I like to have a soundtrack for my life and just have certain songs playing in the background all day. I love epic soundtracks with strings and modern soundtracks that mix pop music with classical scores.

There is something about music that cannot only put you in a certain mood, but can take you to a different place emotionally and spiritually. Whether it's doing the dishes, having some reflective time or working in the yard, I like my time better filled with music.

If you are having a hard time accessing the Presence, sometimes all you need is the right soundtrack.

When you can't pray or think or read your way into God's Presence, then try singing and playing instruments.

The psalmist in Psalm 33 instructs us to sing joyfully to the Lord. He goes on to say that our praise should be musical with instruments. You can play the music of others, or you can make your own. But there is something about expressive, beautiful and passionate music to worship God and bring us into an encounter of the Presence.

In Psalm 33, this praise is going forth because the psalmist is reflecting on the character and nature of who God is. His "Word... is right and true."

"He is faithful in all He does."

"He loves righteousness and justice."

"The earth is full of his unfailing love."

You see, when we look at who God is, we always have a reason to sing and make music to God. Worship is about singing back to God, who has revealed Himself to us in His Word. We can keep singing new songs because there is always more for us to know and discover about who God is.

Listening to new music about who God is and making up our own love songs to Jesus fuels our love for God and inspires us to worship.

As we read above, "it is fitting for the upright to praise Him."

Coach Al Hollingsworth once taught me, "It is easier to act your way into a feeling than to feel your way into an action."

It is fitting for us to praise God even when we don't feel like it, because God is worthy of our praise.

But when we enter into praise with passion and music, we start to feel God and want to know Him more.

———

Lord, I sing to You a new song. You are worthy of all my worship and praise. It is fitting that I should praise You. Let my praise be expressive and filled with music. Give me new songs that touch Your heart and move me to magnify Your name. You are great and the earth is full of Your love. You are faithful in all You do. I love You! In Jesus' name, amen.

My Defender
July 17

Lord, you have seen this; do not be silent. Do not be far from me, Lord. Awake, and rise to my defense! Contend for me, my God and Lord. Vindicate me in your righteousness, Lord my God; do not let them gloat over me.
Psalms 35:22-24

Who has your back?

If you get into trouble in life, who is there to protect you and defend you?

When I was young, a neighbor boy got upset with me and started a fight with me. I can't remember what started it all, but what I *do* remember is my brother coming to be my defender.

The neighbor boy grabbed me, and my brother came up from behind him and got rid of him. Sometimes trouble is the opportunity we need to find out who has our back.

In Psalm 35, David is crying out to God in desperation because he is under attack from his enemies. These are literal enemies plotting and attempting to kill him. These are not just boardroom enemies, an upset neighbor or someone that is against your beliefs. David is literally fearing for his life.

If God can help David in these life-threatening situations, then he can also certainly defend us in the boardroom, with our neighbors or with those who come against us.

David knows that when he is being threatened, the Lord sees him. His prayer is "Do not be far from me."

What is he praying?

He is praying for the Presence.

David knows that God's nearness is what makes the difference.

David is confident that if God is near, then God will be his Defender. God will contend with David's enemies and vindicate him.

We can get through anything when God is near.

God's Presence brings us comfort, peace and favor, but it also brings us protection from our enemies.

We can rely on God in the most difficult circumstances. Great threats do not mean we are abandoned by God, but can become opportunities for us to see that is He is not far from us, and He comes to our rescue.

The Lord is looking upon you, and whoever messes with the righteous will have to deal with God. He is your Defender, and He is near.

Lord, You are my Defender. Be not far from me. Let me know Your Presence. You see the threats of my enemies. Contend for me. Vindicate me. You will not allow my enemies to have the last word. Do not let them gloat over me. Defend me and grant me victory. I love to see how You come to my rescue. In Jesus' name, amen.

Wait Patiently
July 18

Be still before the Lord and wait patiently for him; do not fret when people succeed in their ways, when they carry out their wicked schemes.
Psalms 37:7

Do you ever become bothered when you see unrighteous people get away with things and succeed at their plans?

It can be rather frustrating when we see headlines or even know people directly who are prospering while doing things dishonestly or in corrupt ways.

God has given us a longing for justice. Of course, sin can corrupt our pure pursuit of justice, but God has wired it into us as His creation.

I've been frustrated many times by seeing people get away with things and appear to get ahead of others while doing it.

God has an antidote to our stress over evil in the world. His antidote is the Presence. When we learn to be still before Him and wait patiently for Him, we can enter into a place of rest for our soul.

David is regularly crying out to God about why the evil prosper. David gets honest and shares his true emotions with God, but he learns to transcend how he feels by working through his emotions with God's help.

When we fellowship with God in His Presence, God tends to the cares of our heart.

Grace and I have some friends who often remind us we aren't supposed to carry the weight of the world on our shoulders. They are referring to the widespread access to information we all have through social media and the many ways to get the news now.

We can get a constant stream of news stories to be outraged about.

But how much can we really control the outcome of world events or when people carry out their wicked plans? We need to learn to spend more time in the Presence than to dwell upon things we have no control over.

When we come before God, we need to learn to be still before the Lord. One of the spiritual disciplines Christians have practiced is learning stillness and waiting patiently on God. Many saints throughout the years would take silent retreats to learn to wait on God.

We need to cultivate the discipline of being still before the Lord. Learning to sit before God is a counter-cultural practice of trust in who He is.

While the world is striving to get ahead by their plotting and scheming, the believer gets ahead by slowing down and waiting patiently on the Lord.

We trust the Lord to take care of evil and to take care of our needs.

Lord, forgive me for the times I have given so much energy to negativity and those who do evil in the world. Deliver me from stress and strain. Help me to wait patiently for You and learn to sit in stillness before You. I trust You. You are a righteous judge, and I can depend upon You. In Jesus' name, amen.

As the Deer
July 19

As the deer pants for streams of water, so my soul pants for you, my God. My soul thirsts for God, for the living God. When can I go and meet with God?
Psalms 42:1-2

Have you ever been so dehydrated you would do anything for a drink of water?

We live in the age of so many types of water that are available. There is electrolyte water, alkaline water, reverse osmosis water and flavored water. There is plastic bottled water, glass bottled water and boxed water.

My youngest daughter is convinced that boxed water is the best. Every store is now full of all types of water that promise perfect hydration for the satisfaction of your thirst.

In Psalm 42, the psalmist says he is desperately thirsty for God as a deer pants for streams of water.

I heard a powerful excerpt from Pastor Charlie Dates, who studied this passage as it relates to deer.

Deer can move quickly, but they don't sweat. So, they can overheat when they are on the run from a predator. When a deer cannot get water to cool down, it pants to cool itself. Its panting releases a scent which helps predators find it.

But when a deer gets to the water, it cools itself down and can stay hidden from whatever is hunting it.

People of the Presence are desperate for God and thirst for Him. When you love God so much, you would do anything to get another drink of His Presence. You are like the deer.

Oh, how our souls should long for God. When we thirst for Him and pursue Him until we receive a drink from His Spirit, we are refreshed and hidden from our enemies that pursue us.

The streams or rivers of water in the Scripture speak of the Presence of the Holy Spirit. This Psalmist knew all he needed when he was being pursued or he was tired and weary in life was to meet with God.

To meet with God is to drink of His Presence and receive the quenching of the thirst in our soul. Our need for God is our greatest need in life.

It's not enough to just know we need Him or agree that we need Him, but to pursue Him in our thirst until we are satisfied in Him.

Lord, as the deer pants for streams of water, so my soul pants for You. You are the longing of my heart and soul. I thirst for You, my God, the living God. I long to go and meet with You. There is no one like You. Only You can satisfy my thirsty soul. I love you, Lord. In Jesus' name, amen.

Humbled Us
July 20

But now you have rejected and humbled us; you no longer go out with our armies.
Psalms 44:9

Have you ever been humbled?

I'm trying to think of a time where I have been humbled and, to be honest, it's hard to pick which time to share because there have been so many.

I've been humbled in sports, in leadership, in friendship, in school and at work.

No one likes to eat humble pie, but the results of humility are wonderful.

Pride so easily creeps into our motivation and it makes us feel good about ourselves until the faulty foundation we are on is exposed.

Being humbled for me usually comes with realizing I am wrong and that I need to correct course.

Humility often comes when another person is used by God to show me I am wrong or God makes Himself clear to me in prayer, His Word, or circumstances that I have been caught in pride.

In Psalms 44, the psalmist of the son's of Korah is mourning that God has rejected His people and humbled them.

How does he see the evidence of God's judgement upon them?

How does he know they have been humbled?

Because "You no longer go out with our armies."

In one sense, the psalmist is saying that God isn't with them, so they lose their battles. But in another sense, it's about the Presence being lost, which causes them to lose.

The cry of Moses when God called him to lead Israel to the promised land, and he encountered God's glory was "If You don't go with us, we don't want to go."

Moses longed for the Presence to be with them, or nothing else mattered. Now, in this Psalm, they are mourning because God doesn't go with them any longer.

This is the most humbling thing for the people of God, Israel, because they were to be people of the Presence

We can easily focus on obedience to God out of fear we will get in trouble for breaking the rules. It is not completely wrong to be motivated by wanting to avoid punishment.

But what if our focus was that we didn't want to lose the preciousness of God's Presence, and, therefore, we stay humble?

Our greatest reward, delight, and prize is that God is with us.

He goes with us.

Don't miss out on what matters most: Him.

The most humbling thing God can do is stop going with us and withdraw His Presence.

The greatest thing we can do is stay in a posture of humility to attract His Presence.

———

Lord God, I humble myself before You. I turn from pride and selfishness. I turn from every false way. I don't want to get to a place where You withdraw Your Presence. Keep going out with me. If I have lost Your Presence in any way, I repent and return to You. I treasure Your Presence in my life above all else. In Jesus' name, amen.

Love/Hate

July 21

You love righteousness and hate wickedness; therefore God, your God, has set you above your companions by anointing you with the oil of joy.
Psalms 45:7

Have you ever had a love/hate relationship?
We use this phrase in our culture called love/hate, which seems illogical on the one hand, but represents a relationship we have with certain things in life.

For instance, we might have a love for candy, but we hate how it can have control over us.

We usually use this phrase for something that feels good but has bad consequences. Because sometimes things feel good but are not good for us.

But the truth is, if we love something, we will hate what destroys love.

If you are a lover, then you will have something you hate. If you love someone bound in addiction, then you love the person, but you hate the addiction that destroys their life.

In Psalm 45, the psalmist is speaking about the One who operates in a love/hate relationship. This Psalm is about the secret to Jesus' life and ministry carrying the anointing, or the Presence.

God anointed Jesus the Son of God with the oil of joy because He loved righteousness and hated wickedness.

If we want to have the anointing like Jesus, we must love righteousness and hate wickedness as well.

The anointing, as we looked at earlier in this series, is the oil that was smeared upon holy people and holy objects that came from crushed and pressed olives. The anointing oil is representative of the Presence of the Holy Spirit for consecration, empowerment, and service.

Those who are of the Presence are smeared with the oil that comes from crushing and pressing. This crushing and pressing releases in us a love for righteousness and a hatred for wickedness.

If we want to attract the anointing or the Presence, then we need to develop a mind and a life that is attractive to God. Of course, we can only be holy by the grace of God and receive His Presence as a gift. I am not talking about earning. I am talking about obedience and the formation of our desires to be formed by the desires of the One we love.

If we love Jesus, we ought to love what He loves and hate what He hates.

When grace is operating in us, we bear this fruit of obedience.

To be anointed with joy means we have been set above our companions.

God's reward for our love of righteousness and a hatred for wickedness is the anointing. The Presence is both our pursuit and our prize.

Lord Jesus, You love righteousness and hate wickedness, therefore God has set You above all others and anointed You with the oil of joy. Make my life like Yours. Anoint me with the oil of joy. Through the pressing and crushing of learning to love righteousness and hate wickedness, You release Your Presence over me. You are my pursuit, and You are my prize. In Your name, Jesus, amen.

Stillness in Trouble
July 22

God is our refuge and strength, an ever-present help in trouble. Therefore we will not fear, though the earth give way and the mountains fall into the heart of the sea, though its waters roar and foam and the mountains quake with their surging. There is a river whose streams make glad the city of God, the holy place where the Most High dwells. God is within her, she will not fall; God will help her at break of day. Nations are in uproar, kingdoms fall; he lifts his voice, the earth melts.
He says, "Be still, and know that I am God; I will be exalted among the nations, I will be exalted in the earth.
Psalms 46:1-6, 10

Have you ever heard of a panic room?

A panic room is a safe place in a house or building where people can enter and secure themselves in case of some danger or trouble.

I've never seen a panic room. I don't like the name of it because its name sounds so hopeless and fear inspiring.

We all need a safe place to turn to when events arise that can cause panic. Maybe not a literal safe room, but we all need a place that is safe for our mind and soul.

In Psalm 46, a Psalm of the sons of Korah, we are reminded that God Himself is even better than a panic room. He is our refuge, strength and fortress.

We don't need to live in fear during times of trouble. This Psalm describes both natural calamities and political upheaval. Whether it's earthquakes or wars and violence, God is our protector and place of safety.

Being in the Presence is not only a place of safety but also a place of refreshing and joy. The Presence is a place where "The river whose streams make glad the city of God" make the heart of the believer glad in Him.

All this talk of God being our refuge and strength is Presence language, where we go and dwell alone with Him.

The psalmist takes things further, though. For God to be our safe place and for us to experience the river of God, the place of the Presence of the Spirit, we have to learn how to be a people who "Be still and know that He is God."

Stillness in God's Presence is a daily discipline we need to learn to cultivate.

Everything can be going crazing in the world, and where people would typically panic, a person of the Presence has learned to cultivate a stillness that is stronger than the rage of nature and nations.

Stillness is a discipline of waiting on God.

Read the Bible. Sing a song. Keep things simple.

Sit quietly before the Lord in His Presence.

Build a lifestyle of sitting in stillness in His Presence and you can sit in stillness with God in times of trouble.

Lord God, You are my dwelling place. You are my refuge and strength. You are my fortress. Teach me how to sit before You in stillness, that I might know You are God. Help me in my time with You to sit before You and wait and listen. In Jesus' name, amen.

Awaken the Dawn
July 23

My heart, O God, is steadfast, my heart is steadfast; I will sing and make music. Awake, my soul! Awake, harp and lyre! I will awaken the dawn.
Psalms 57:7-8

Do you usually wake up early enough to see the sunrise?

I'm more of a morning person than I used to be, and that might be because we moved into a home where we can really see the beauty of the sunrise. Grace and I love to wake up in the morning and open our curtains to see what kind of painting God created across the horizon during the sunset.

On a clear day, we can see the sun come up from behind the mountains and shades of blue, purple, pink, orange and yellow in different varying combinations ripple across the sky.

There is something beautiful and invigorating about starting the day with a breathtaking sunrise.

The thing about the sunrise is that the sun wakes you up to start the day. But in Psalm 57, David says that he is going to awaken the dawn. The dawn is the first light that is building towards the sunrise.

He's not waiting for the sunrise to happen to him. He is about to awaken the new day!

We can only enter the Presence at God's will and invitation. We can't make God manifest for us by our own volition. But we also learn from David that we have to make a decision to worship and trust in God, even in times of great testing.

David says that his heart is steadfast and no matter what, he will sing and make music. He says, "Awake, my soul!"

David speaks to himself to awaken and make music.

Entering the Presence is initiated by God. We enter not by our feelings, but a choice that we will worship and praise to enter into His dwelling place.

Don't wait to feel like worshiping. Choose to put God first, early in the day!

I would like to be better about early prayer. So many things can interrupt plans later in the day.

Tell your soul you are going to awake and praise God!

Decide that today is a day for the Presence!

Today is a day to awaken the dawn!

Tell yourself, "Soul, you will worship God! Awake, my soul! Enter into God's dwelling place! You will sing and praise the Lord!"

To some degree we get to choose what kind of day we are going to have.

Choose to awaken the dawn rather than let the sunrise awaken you.

Be intentional about the Presence and let your heart be steadfast in worship as you seek Him, your refuge.

O God, my heart is steadfast in You. I worship You. I will sing and make music for You. There is no one like You. Awake, my soul! I will awaken the dawn! Help me to pray early and pray first. My soul, You will sing and praise and seek the Lord, early will You seek Him. In Jesus' name, amen.

The Higher Rock
July 24

Hear my cry, O God; listen to my prayer. From the ends of the earth I call to you, I call as my heart grows faint; lead me to the rock that is higher than I. For you have been my refuge, a strong tower against the foe. I long to dwell in your tent forever and take refuge in the shelter of your wings.
Psalms 61:1-4

Have you ever wanted to be somewhere desperately, but you didn't have access to enter that location? Such as, getting in to meet a person of power or fame, or a sold-out sporting event or concert?

If you were ever denied such an opportunity initially, but then somehow you got in, it was most likely because you knew a person who made it so.

As the saying goes, "It's not what you know, it's who you know."

The Presence can only be reached by the Lord making the way for you.

The NIV study Bible says about this passage: "The place of security that he seeks is beyond his reach; only God can bring him to it." *

David is crying out to God to get him to the rock that is higher than him. But He needs God's leadership to get him to the place he longs to dwell.

God listens to our cries and our prayers. No matter how bleak things are in life, He listens to us, especially our cry to be with Him.

The rock speaks of Christ. The New Testament confirms to us that Jesus is our rock. We don't come to Him on our own will. Jesus came to us to make a way into God's Presence.

Psalm 61 is a picture of this truth that God leads us to the place of safety. He is the way, provides the way, and leads the way.

We can't make it on the level we are at. We need a higher place, a place of refuge. The higher place is a place of salvation, a place where we are protected by our dwelling with the Lord.

David wanted to dwell in God's tent, the tabernacle where God's manifest Presence and glory dwelt. This was the place of the Presence, where we are protected in the shadow of God's wings.

People of the Presence long to be with God now, and long to be with Him forever. Do you hear the longing and passion in the voice of David? He needs God. He aches for His Presence. He knows from where his protection and salvation comes.

Lord Jesus, You are the Rock that is higher than I. I cry out to You. Lead me to Your dwelling place. You are my strong tower and my refuge. There is no one like You. I long to dwell with You forever. Draw me close to the shelter of Your wings. In Your name, amen.

Pour Out Your Heart
July 25

Yes, my soul, find rest in God; my hope comes from him. Truly he is my rock and my salvation; he is my fortress, I will not be shaken. My salvation and my honor depend on God; he is my mighty rock, my refuge. Trust in him at all times, you people; pour out your hearts to him, for God is our refuge.
Psalms 62:5-8

Do you have a friend who you can trust with all your secrets?

I remember as a youth, one of our summer camp speakers, Darren Lindley, would challenge many times to live a life without secrets. He was careful to say we didn't need to tell everyone our secrets, but we needed to find someone we could trust with the confession of our sin and the sharing of our pain.

Of course, you need to have a high degree of trust in someone to share your secrets with them. Being able to pour your heart out and not keep things bottled up inside is a very healing experience.

David is writing in Psalm 62 about how we can find true rest for our soul in God. God is a safe place for us to run to in dangerous times. God is a refuge and a fortress. We can depend upon Him. A theme we have talked about a lot in this series on the Presence is God being our refuge.

This is a theme that is repeated by David over and over. In Psalm 62, David adds something unique about God being our refuge. He says, "Pour out your hearts to Him."

Since David said we can trust God at all times as our refuge, he says specifically we can trust God with our hearts.

At the time of this writing, I just finished a conference at our church. David Wagner, one of our speakers, talked about how God wanted to heal people's hope and deliver them from "death by a thousand disappointments."

I watched as people responded to him and the ministry of Leif Hetland in this instance. It was so simple, and a gentle time in the Presence.

People came and poured out their hearts to God, while others surrounded them and prayed with them. There was such an intensely sweet weeping that occurred in the room as people received the healing love of God.

You can trust God with your hurts, disappointments, and your sin. Don't bottle things up. Your secrets are hurting you. God's Presence is a place of total transparency where you can bare your soul and pour your heart about before Him. This place where you meet with God in raw honesty is the place where He protects your heart and heals your soul to find rest in Him.

Father God, I come to You as my refuge and my fortress. I want to dwell with You. My soul finds rest in You alone. Where I have not been able to trust others and have hope, I pray You would heal my hope and my trust. I pour out all my heart to You. Heal me in Your love. In Jesus' name, amen.

Thirsty

July 26

You, God, are my God, earnestly I seek you; I thirst for you, my whole being longs for you, in a dry and parched land where there is no water. I have seen you in the sanctuary and beheld your power and your glory. Because your love is better than life, my lips will glorify you. I will praise you as long as I live, and in your name I will lift up my hands.
Psalms 63:1-4

What is the most desperate you have ever been for water? Have you ever experienced thirst so intensely that your life depended on it?

I know playing sports has got to leave you parched at certain times. But preaching has probably made me even more thirsty than playing sports. However, I can't recall any times where I have been so thirsty that my life has depended upon it.

There are places in the world where access to good, clean water is not available and people have thirsted to death. You can live for weeks without food, but you can only live a few days without water.

In Psalm 63, David is in a life-threatening situation again. In this dangerous situation in the desert, David is longing for God like he is longing for water.

David uses the desperation of his situation as fuel for his devotion to God. David longs and thirsts for God like a dying man in a desert longs for water.

David remembers the power and glory of being in God's sanctuary.

What is David saying?

He remembers the Presence. He is desperate for the Presence of God as a dying man in a desert is thirsty for water.

David knows that God's love is even better than life.

David has a holy ache to dwell with God.

David has the discipline to practice the Presence even when his life is on the line.

He thirsts to be with God more than anything.

David knows that water will satisfy him, but there is a greater longing that David has to be satisfied with God Himself.

We are all longing for God whether we know it or not.

Do we love God like David?

Do we long for God like David?

Are we thirsty for God more than we are thirsty for water?

Is the Presence the greatest pursuit of our lives?

Let us worship and long for Him like a dying man thirsts for water in a dry and parched land.

Lord Jesus, I thirst for You. I long to dwell with You. I repent for longing for anything more than I long for You. There is nothing in this world that can satisfy me like Your Presence. Your love is better than my life. I praise You and lift my hands before You. In Your name, amen.

The Blessing of Nearness
July 27

Blessed are those you choose and bring near to live in your courts! We are filled with the good things of your house, of your holy temple. The whole earth is filled with awe at your wonders; where morning dawns, where evening fades, you call forth songs of joy.
Psalms 65:4, 8

Have you ever been chosen, and it made you feel special?

I had a boss who confided in me and chose me for certain tasks. He often spoke of my good qualities and encouraged me. It really helped shape me as a young man to be chosen when he needed a sounding board or needed help troubleshooting a situation for the business.

It's a blessing to be chosen to be a part of someone's inner circle.

David shares the greatest blessing, the blessing of nearness. He says we are blessed when we are chosen by God to live near His courts.

It's one thing to be chosen by people we respect, but quite another to be chosen by God. And not just chosen by God in a general sense but chosen by Him to dwell near Him.

This is the inheritance of the Presence.

Later, David talks about how the whole earth is full of God's wonder. We see in the dawn and in the fading of the evening that there is a wonder that inspires us to worship. All throughout creation, we can access God's Presence in worship as we marvel at the beauty of His creation.

We can access God's nearness from any point in the earth.

God dwells in all the earth, but there is a nearness we can enjoy by dwelling near His house.

The earth is filled with awe at God's wonders, but we can be filled with the good things of God's house. We cannot only observe the Presence; we can be filled with the Presence and dwell near our God of wonders.

God initiates the way into His Presence.

Never take for granted how He invites you with the blessing of being near Him. There is no greater blessing than the nearness of the Presence.

Lord God, You inspire worship at the wonder of Your creation. You are seen everywhere in this beautiful world which You have made. As I worship You with songs of joy, You invite me to dwell near Your house. There is no greater blessing than the nearness of Your Presence. Let me live near Your courts. I love the place Your glory dwells. In Jesus' name, amen.

Shout!
July 28

Shout for joy to God, all the earth! Sing the glory of his name; make his praise glorious. Say to God, "How awesome are your deeds! So great is your power that your enemies cringe before you. All the earth bows down to you; they sing praise to you, they sing the praises of your name.
Psalms 66:1-4

Have you ever lost your voice from shouting?
I'm a talker and I get loud, so I've lost my voice a lot in church, in sporting events and in concerts. I love to shout in worship and I'm not good at pacing myself when I preach.

I used to lose my voice every Sunday from preaching with passion, but also because I loved to sing loud during the worship. I love getting to sing at the top of my lungs with one of my favorite bands or music artists. There is something about putting your whole heart and your whole body into a shout!

In Psalm 66, we are instructed to "Shout for joy to God!"
We are to sing in a way that makes our praise glorious.

We are to declare how awesome God is and lift up His name.

Making our praise loud is a key to entering God's Presence.

There are times when we are to be still and peaceful to access God's presence. But there is something about shouting our praise loudly that also causes us to enter the Presence.

Later in this Psalm, we learn that if we don't deal with sin in our heart, God will not hear us. Dwelling in God's presence requires more than outward expressions of worship; it is important to have a right heart.

But when our heart is right before Him, a good shout for joy has the power to affect our enemies, our environment, and our access to God's manifest Presence.

If you haven't shouted in a time of worship, get ready to turn it up in your time alone with Him or when you worship with your church. Put your whole heart and your whole voice into some holy and happy shouts. Bring God your whole heart and lift up a sound. Don't care what others think about you being bold in worship.

Of course, don't draw attention towards yourself in a gathering of worship, but also don't hold back. Bringing God a shout of praise is glorious, liberating, and changes the atmosphere.

Lord, I shout for joy to You, my God! I sing and shout and bring You praise! Your power causes my enemies to cringe! Show me how to make Your praise glorious! You are worthy! I will not regard sin in my heart, so that You will receive my prayer. I enter boldly and loudly into Your Presence, My King! In Jesus' name, amen!

Shine On Us
July 29

May God be gracious to us and bless us and make his face shine on us— so that your ways may be known on earth, your salvation among all nations.
Psalms 67:1-2

Who do you let get in your face?

Letting someone in your face is a sign of trust and intimacy. We don't let strangers in our faces.

My wife can come close to my face because she is my favorite. My kids can come close to my face. As I got older, my dad even returned to coming close to my face and kissing my cheek.

We don't let just anyone in our face. The closer someone can come to my face, the closer the relationship.

Psalm 67 is a song and a prayer that God would be gracious and bless us and make His face shine upon us. The greatest blessing God can give us is to bring us close to His face and cause His face to shine on us.

The Presence being manifest in our lives is about the nearness of

God's face. We can't see His face and have Him shine upon us unless we are close.

When we trust God, we let Him close. God wants intimacy with us. He is gracious to us. When He is our God and we have put our trust in Him, our inheritance is the nearness of His face. There is a quality of relationship that God longs to share with us.

It's sad to think that many Christians can know about God but not experience the shine that comes from His face. God is so gracious to share Himself with us and make Himself available to us. He wants to be close.

This kind of nearness with God, where His face shines upon us, has the power to change the world. The psalmist said that when His face shines on us, God's ways are known to the whole world and salvation to all nations.

God's plan to reach the world is about a people that are distinctively graced with the Presence. This writer knew that when God's glory rests upon us, we will have influence in the world.

This has been my prayer more and more, that I would see God's face. I don't want to be distant. I long to dwell in a close relationship where His face shines upon me. I want to shift the atmosphere in my city.

True transformation comes not just from hard work and strategy, it comes from radiating the shine of His face to those who need God most. Reaching the nations is a Presence project. Come in close to let His face shine upon you.

God, be gracious to me and bless me and make Your face shine on me. I want to see Your ways known on all the earth and Your salvation among the nations. Let me be a carrier of Your Presence. I trust You and I thank You that You want to bring me near to Your face. Let the shine of Your face mold me and shape me. I love the glory of Your face. In Jesus' name, amen.

Better is One Day
July 30

How lovely is your dwelling place, Lord Almighty! My soul yearns, even faints, for the courts of the Lord; my heart and my flesh cry out for the living God. Better is one day in your courts than a thousand elsewhere; I would rather be a doorkeeper in the house of my God than dwell in the tents of the wicked.
Psalms 84:1-2, 10

Have you ever been to a concert with crazy fans?
I've been to concerts with pretty crazy fans, but I've heard stories about fans that are so crazy they would pass out from excitement and screaming.

Whether it's the Beetles or 90s boy bands, fans would get so loud that concert goers could not even hear the band they came to see. People can get so passionate about getting close to someone who inspires them.

In Psalm 84, the psalmist is passionate about God.

This is lover language. The writers of the Psalms were lovers of God, lovers of the Presence.

His soul yearns and even faints to be near the Lord Almighty. His heart and his flesh are desperate for God's Presence. He knows the experience of the Presence that even touches his flesh, his body.

This manifest Presence of God not only touches the soul, it touches his flesh.

As the Psalm continues, he declares that it's better to have one day in the courts of the Lord than to have a thousand days elsewhere. The cry of this song comes from someone who prioritizes the Presence.

We can have many great days in many places, but nothing compares with just one day in the Presence of God. He would rather be a doorkeeper in the house of God than to dwell anywhere else.

People of the Presence reject the value that comes from title or position over the prize of being with God. It doesn't matter if his position is a doorkeeper, just to be near is what matters.

I don't want to become a professional Christian or professional pastor. I want the simple longing and desperation that comes from a lover's heart for God.

The reason I followed God is because He loved me and pursued me when I was in such desperate need for help. Only His Presence could satisfy me.

I don't want to ever lose the longing for one day in His house.

One day with Him is better than all others.

Lord, I love Your dwelling place more than all others! My soul yearns and faints to be with You. My heart and flesh cry out for You, Almighty God. Better is one day with You than a thousand elsewhere. I consider every title and position in life inferior to being Your lover God. Just to be near the place Your glory dwells is the longing of my heart. In Jesus' name, amen.

Hide Your Face?
July 31

*But I cry to you for help, Lord; in the morning my prayer comes before you.
Why, Lord, do you reject me and hide your face from me?
Psalms 88:13-14*

Have you ever lost contact with someone close to you?
One of the hardest things in life is the absence of a friend or a loved one. The greatest ache in my life has been the loss of friendships to death or distance.

Sometimes I've lost friendships due to betrayal or misunderstandings. I've come to learn the presence or absence of a friend is the greatest joy or sorrow in my life.

When I have friendships, I have true riches.

The psalmist in Psalm 88 is mourning the loss of the Presence. He declares that he calls out to God for help every morning. But He has lost the sense of God's nearness.

He says, "Why, Lord, do you reject me and hide your face from me?"

This stings the psalmist. He is grieved over the fact that He doesn't see the face of God anymore.

The Israelites were to be a people of the Presence. This brought the favor of God's face upon them.

Some of the Psalms are a song of mourning over what the people of God had lost when they turned to rebellion and faced God's judgment. The greatest judgement of all is the absence of His Presence.

But what if we saw the devastation and the brokenness of our families, neighborhoods and cities as places that are devoid of God's Presence?

What if every broken area in the world just needs God to be near?

There is something about this cry for help to the Lord that is beautiful. It acknowledges the true value of His nearness.

There are things in the world we need to grieve over.

I like to focus on the victory we have in Christ and live in hope.

We serve a God of redemption who loves to do miracles in our lives.

But there are times where things have gone really bad in life and in society and we should ache for the return of God's face to smile upon us again.

Lord God, I know there is more of You. I want to see Your face. I want more of Your Presence. But there are times where I feel rejected and that Your face is hidden from me and my people. Do not hide Your face from me, my family or my city. Let Your Presence be upon us. Let Your Presence be upon my nation. Your nearness is our greatest need. In Jesus' name, amen.

The Secret Place
August 1

He who dwells in the secret place of the Most High Shall abide under the shadow of the Almighty.
Psalms 91:1 NKJV

Have you ever had a teacher teach you something that stuck with you the rest of your life?

As a high school senior at my Christian school, I missed part of Bible class in the mornings because of a firefighting program at another school. My Bible teacher, Mr. Tuggle, assigned me extra Bible verse memory work for the time that I missed every day. He had me memorize Psalm 91 and Psalm 139.

Psalm 91 would become one of the most important chapters of the Bible in my life when I went through a time of dealing with shame, depression, and anxiety in my early twenties.

Psalm 91 is all about the one who dwells in the secret place. The Psalmist declares that God is in the secret place and the place of protection for the believer. To me it is the most powerful of all the Psalms on the Presence.

But the blessings promised in this Psalm are all conditional to verse 1, "He who dwells in the secret place..."

You have to be a Presence dweller, one who spends time alone with God to receive all that He has for you.

Use this Psalm as a prayer.

Declare it.

Make war with it against whatever assaults your heart and mind.

Confess it.

Meditate upon it.

As this chapter washes over you, you will be drawn to the Presence and filled with confidence that comes from living under the "shadow of the Almighty."

This passage set me free and gave me the courage to overcome so much negative thinking. I pray it does the same for you!

"He who dwells in the secret place of the Most High Shall abide under the shadow of the Almighty. I will say of the Lord, "He is my refuge and my fortress; My God, in Him I will trust." Surely He shall deliver you from the snare of the fowler And from the perilous pestilence. He shall cover you with His feathers, And under His wings you shall take refuge; His truth shall be your shield and buckler. You shall not be afraid of the terror by night, Nor of the arrow that flies by day, Nor of the pestilence that walks in darkness, Nor of the destruction that lays waste at noonday. A thousand may fall at your side, And ten thousand at your right hand; But it shall not come near you. Only with your eyes shall you look, And see the reward of the wicked. Because you have made the Lord, who is my refuge, Even the Most High, your dwelling place, No evil shall befall you, Nor shall any plague come near your dwelling; For He shall give His angels charge over you, To keep you in all your ways. In their hands they shall bear you up, Lest you dash your foot against a stone. You shall tread upon the lion and the cobra, The young lion and the serpent you shall trample underfoot.

"Because he has set his love upon Me, therefore I will deliver him; I will set him on high, because he has known My name. He shall call upon Me, and I will answer him; I will be with him in trouble; I will deliver him and honor him. With long life I will satisfy him, And show him My salvation." In Jesus' name amen! Psalms 91:1-16 NKJV

How We Come
August 2

Oh come, let us sing to the Lord! Let us shout joyfully to the Rock of our salvation. Let us come before His presence with thanksgiving; Let us shout joyfully to Him with psalms. For the Lord is the great God, And the great King above all gods.
Psalms 95:1-3 NKJV

What is your favorite place to sing?
Do you like to sing in the shower?
How about in the church?
I love to have a song in my heart at all times.

I walk around my house and the church and I'm almost always singing or humming some tune of praise. My favorite place to worship God, though, is with live music.

My wife and I both love a packed room that shouts and sings with a spirit of celebration to glorify the Lord. There is nothing like a group of people in love with Jesus that boldly express their thanks in joyful songs.

In Psalm 95, we are instructed to sing and to sing joyfully to the Lord, the Rock of our salvation.

Then comes the revelation on the Presence. We "come before His Presence with thanksgiving."

This is how we come before Him.

This is how we draw near.

We bring God songs of joyful thanksgiving.

Because He is the great God and the great King above all gods.

How we come before Him matters.

He has given us a way to enter His Presence: Thanksgiving.

Grumbling and complaining will not draw the anointing and nearness of the Holy Spirit.

Griping and whining is not the way.

But being thankful in any situation has the power to bring you before the Presence. This is God's instruction for us to experience His manifest Presence.

We thank God because of who He is.

I've been through difficult battles with disease and discouragement, and you know what?

He is still worthy of praise.

I can experience Him in any season when I stay thankful. We always have a reason to sing when we think about the One who is "the great King above all gods."

My soul rejoices in this King when I think about how wonderful and powerful my God is. I just want to sing and thank Him.

Oh, how quickly He draws near and touches my heart with His Presence. I feel His warmth and I never want His Presence to leave.

In songs of thanksgiving, this is how we come before His Presence!

Lord Jesus, You are the Rock of my salvation! You are the great King above all gods! You surpass them all! I shout to You and sing to You with joy. You are my everything. I thank You for my life and for Your grace. Thank You for being my God. Reveal more of Yourself to me that I might praise You more and more! In Jesus' name, amen!

The New Song and the Beauty of Holiness
August 3

Oh, sing to the Lord a new song! Sing to the Lord, all the earth. Sing to the Lord, bless His name; Proclaim the good news of His salvation from day to day. Oh, worship the Lord in the beauty of holiness! Tremble before Him, all the earth.
Psalms 96:1-2, 9 NKJV

What is it about a new song that can really touch your heart? I almost don't know how to put into words how a new song can impact me like nothing else. There have been certain worship songs and songs from other genres of music that have inspired, healed, strengthened and ignited creativity in me the first time I heard them. I can sit and listen to new songs and artists enough to get on the nerves of my family. I love to get lost in an endless stream of music. Discovering new songs that touch your heart, express your current emotions and glorify God can be a soaring experience in the Presence of God.

We are exhorted in Psalm 96 to sing a new song! Being in the church my whole life, I've been exposed to so many different styles of music and songs we sing that span decades. I love when new songs are introduced to the church.

Some Christians complain of new songs being introduced, but it is very important to keep introducing new ones to keep our worship fresh and engaging. Of course, we can't do new songs all the time and there is value in repeating songs from the past.

But new songs mean fresh inspiration about who God is in our life!

We worship God not only with new songs but also in the beauty of holiness. We need variety in our expression of love to God, but we need to be faithful in our character.

Our worship that comes from a holy heart is beautiful to the Lord. When we see God in greater depths and gain new understanding of who He is, we sing new songs about Him.

We enter into the Presence in this place and tremble before Him.

New songs and worship in holiness are a recipe for encounters with the Divine Presence of God.

Make up a new song and sing it to God.

Discover some new worship music and begin to sing God's truth with your whole heart.

Get ready for an encounter with God.

Press into worship until you tremble before Him.

He is worthy of new expressions of worship songs and worship in the beauty of holiness!

Lord, I sing a new song to You! Release a new song among all the people of the earth! Let us proclaim Your salvation with new melodies and praises. You are worthy! I worship You in the beauty of holiness. Let me experience Your Presence until I tremble before You. In Jesus' name, amen.

Seek Him with All Your Heart

August 4

I seek you with all my heart; do not let me stray from your commands.
Psalms 119:10

Have you ever had a rewarding punishment?

One my mentors and a man of God that has been like a spiritual father to me, Dr. Thomas, tells the story of when he got in trouble as a little boy.

His Dad's punishment before he could eat dinner was to write out one Psalm.

He wrote Psalm 117, which is the shortest Psalm of all the Psalms.

When his dad saw he took the easy way, the next night, he had him write out Psalm 119, which is the longest of all the Psalms. It is 168 verses long.

It was his consequence, but it was also a reward to spend that much time with such a rich psalm.

Psalm 119 is all about seeking God with all your heart through a love and reverence for the Word of God.

The words "law, statutes, precepts, promise, decrees, commands, word and ways" are repeated over and over throughout the entire Psalm.

This Psalm is all about longing for God and an utter dependence upon His Word.

This is where we see there is a clear connection between the Presence and the Word of God.

To sustain a life in the Presence, have a sustained life in the Scriptures.

Meditate on these nuggets from Psalm 119 (NIV):
>   See him with all their heart (v. 2)
>   My soul is consumed with longing... (v. 20)
>   You are My portion Lord (v. 57)
>   The earth is filled with Your love Lord (v. 64)
>   My soul faints with longing for Your salvation (v. 81)
>   Your word is a lamp for my feet, a light to my path (v. 105)
>   You are my refuge and my shield; I have put my hope in Your word (v. 114)
>   ...Your commands give me delight (v. 143)
>   ...My heart trembles at Your word (v. 161)
>   I rejoice in Your promise like one who finds great spoil (v. 162)
>   Let me live that I might praise You (v. 175)

I've found that when my soul is dry and I long for His Presence, as I exalt His Word, He is quick to meet with me.

Oh, how rich is the flood of His peace and Presence when you are honest before the Lord and pour out the longings of your heart! Especially as you cling to the preciousness of His wonderful Word!

Lord, You are my refuge and my shield. Your love fills the whole earth. You are always present, but You manifest Yourself as I exalt Your word and submit to You in my life. I love Your holy Word as I long for You. You are my delight and my joy. There is nothing like Your Presence because there is no one like You. In Jesus' name, amen.

THE MAGNIFIED
AUGUST 5

I will worship toward Your holy temple, And praise Your name For Your lovingkindness and Your truth; For You have magnified Your word above all Your name.
Psalms 138:2 NKJV

How could God magnify His Word above His name?
    I remember teaching on Psalm 138 at a youth camp for a Christian school. A high school student who spent his whole life in church almost could not believe verse two said, "You have magnified Your word above all Your name."

I had to reassure it was actually in the Bible.

This Psalm drove me into the Presence and gave me help when I had broken down in my twenties more than any Psalm besides Psalm 91. I learned to trust in God's name because I grew to trust His Word.

How could God's Word be magnified as greater than His name?

Well, I believe it is very simple. Someone's name is only as good as their word. If God's Word is magnified above all His name, it means that we get to know, experience and trust Him based on what He says.

We only know His name because of His Word.

I learned I can praise before Him, and as I trust His Word, He hears my cries and makes me bold with strength in my soul.

His glory is great.

As I am lowly, He regards me. He revives me in trouble and stretches out His hand against my enemies.

His right hand saves me, and He perfects what concerns me.

My cry is for Him to never forsake me.

Oh, how I love His nearness.

Make this Psalm your prayer today:

———

I will praise You with my whole heart; Before the gods I will sing praises to You. I will worship toward Your holy temple, And praise Your name For Your lovingkindness and Your truth; For You have magnified Your word above all Your name. In the day when I cried out, You answered me, And made me bold with strength in my soul. All the kings of the earth shall praise You, O Lord, When they hear the words of Your mouth. Yes, they shall sing of the ways of the Lord, For great is the glory of the Lord. Though the Lord is on high, Yet He regards the lowly; But the proud He knows from afar. Though I walk in the midst of trouble, You will revive me; You will stretch out Your hand Against the wrath of my enemies, And Your right hand will save me. The Lord will perfect that which concerns me; Your mercy, O Lord, endures forever; Do not forsake the works of Your hands. In Jesus name, amen! Psalms 138:1-8 NKJV

PRESENCE WARFARE
AUGUST 6

May the praise of God be in their mouths and a double-edged sword in their hands, to inflict vengeance on the nations and punishment on the peoples, to bind their kings with fetters, their nobles with shackles of iron, to carry out the sentence written against them— this is the glory of all his faithful people. Praise the Lord.
Psalms 149:6-9

Are you aware that you are in a spiritual war?

It can be very easy to go through life in the western world and quickly forget there is much more than a material world we are dealing with every day.

Praise was a weapon that I used to fight against the voices that warred against my mind in my early twenties.

Reminders of my past sin, floods of shameful memories and hopeless taunts about my future were constantly paraded across my mind.

But when I worshipped with my whole heart at the top of my lungs, I would breakthrough the negative strongholds and find peace in the manifest Presence of God.

In Psalm 149, we read about the power of praise to disrupt the powers in the heavens. This is Presence warfare.

The Bible describes the unseen realm as a place where demons battle God and angels to affect our world and attempt to disrupt the plan of the Almighty for all of us.

This is a real battle that has taken place since the fall of Lucifer at the beginning of humanity.

In the Bible, demonic powers and evil spirits power is tied to the ideas of kings, rulers and nations. They are the evil forces behind governments, leaders, and people who oppose God.

Jesus has defeated Satan and his minions through the cross. His defeat of the evil powers in spiritual places is complete and Satan's future total destruction is imminent.

One of the weapons we have to fight against the influence of evil in our lives and the nations is the weapon of our praise.

The Presence we experience in worship is peace for us, but violence in the spiritual realm against our enemies of death and destruction.

Our praise is powerful.

Our praise, our singing and shouting to God, our dance and the lifting of our hands as acts of adoration have power to stop demons in their tracks.

Our praise can break off depression, lift heaviness, change atmospheres and affect the outcome of our cities and nations.

Singing love songs to God is not just a nice little spiritual exercise but also a release of God's authority over our lives and over critical issues facing the ruling of nations.

Praise is our inheritance, "the glory of His faithful people," to release Presence warfare and affect the outcome of families, cities and nations.

Lord, I bring You my praise! You bind the evil one as I lift You up! Jesus, You are victorious and mighty! You defeated evil, demons and death on the cross! I exalt Your name. There is no one like You. Be exalted over my life, over my city and over my nation. I declare Your greatness over every evil foe, and I exalt Your name. You are worthy of my praise. In Your mighty name, amen!

Everything Praise
August 7

Praise the Lord. Praise God in his sanctuary; praise him in his mighty heavens. Praise him for his acts of power; praise him for his surpassing greatness. Praise him with the sounding of the trumpet, praise him with the harp and lyre, praise him with timbrel and dancing, praise him with the strings and pipe, praise him with the clash of cymbals, praise him with resounding cymbals. Let everything that has breath praise the Lord. Praise the Lord.
Psalms 150:1-6

Do you know someone good at imitating voices?

Growing up I used to try and imitate voices of famous actors. I thought it was so cool to sound like someone else.

My wife can do some voice imitations pretty well. She can sound so perfectly like her mom and her aunts. I know it might not seem that hard to sound like a blood relative, but she does it so perfectly it's hilarious.

As much as someone can sound like someone else, no two voices are exactly alike.

The final Psalm in the Bible, Psalm 150, is all about praise!

Praise the Lord in heaven and in His sanctuary. Praise Him for His acts and for His surpassing greatness. We are to praise Him with every instrument: horns, strings, drums, and pipes. Everything that has breath is to praise the Lord!

Every instrument has a unique sound and everything and everyone who has breath has a unique sound. The drums, the cymbals, the trumpet, the flute and the harp all have a certain breath. The many types of birds, the lions, the dogs, the cats, the frogs, the crickets and the seals all have a different sound from their breath.

And every human has a unique language and a unique voice that brings a unique sound of praise to the Lord.

The whole earth can release a sound of praise that brings God glory and delight. Your sound of praise is unique from your breath.

Everything that has breath and makes a sound can be used as an instrument of praise to celebrate our Creator and enjoy the Presence. Let us use our voice and every expression to praise God for who He is and what He does. He is worthy of all our praise!

Lord, let everything that has breath praise Your holy name! I praise You for Your mighty acts and for Your surpassing greatness! There is no one like You! I bring You joyful songs and celebratory sounds! You are worthy to be praised! In Jesus' name, amen!

Who May Dwell?

August 8

Lord, who may dwell in your sacred tent? Who may live on your holy mountain?
Psalms 15:1

Have you ever had to qualify for something?

My kids are in a speech and debate league. They are talented speakers. To qualify for nationals, they have to perform their speeches and debates according to a certain set of criteria and outperform their competitors.

I had to qualify for certain events in my life related to my education, and of course, there are certain qualifications for me to be in the ministry.

Psalm 15 of David is a list of qualifications for who may dwell in the Presence or in God's sacred tent, the tabernacle where God's glory abides.

The qualifications of who may dwell are:

> *The one whose walk is blameless,*
> *who does what is righteous,*
> *who speaks the truth from their heart;*
> *whose tongue utters no slander,*
> *who does no wrong to a neighbor, and casts no slur on others;*
> *who despises a vile person but honors those who fear the Lord;*
> *who keeps an oath even when it hurts, and does not change their mind;*
> *who lends money to the poor without interest;*
> *who does not accept a bribe against the innocent.*
> *Whoever does these things will never be shaken.*
> *Psalms 15:2-5*

This list of character qualifications to enter God's Presence is a description of a perfect person. Jesus Christ is truly the only blameless man who deserves to dwell in the Presence. But through faith in Christ and abiding in Him, we are invited into this life of character and dwelling in the Presence. Where we cannot earn God's manifest Presence, we can live a life by the grace of Christ Jesus that is attractive to hosting God's glory.

Lord Jesus, through Your blameless life You made the way for me to dwell in God's glorious Presence. Let me be a man who is blameless and upright before You. I want to dwell where You are. Let me be a man who is never shaken, a man who lives in holiness and nearness to You. In Your name, amen.

TO AND FRO
AUGUST 9

For the eyes of the Lord run to and fro throughout the whole earth, to show Himself strong on behalf of those whose heart is loyal to Him.
II Chronicles 16:9 NKJV

Have you ever been pursued?

I have been pursued for promotions and job offers.

It feels good to know that someone has their eye on you.

Of course, people are at times pursued by a romantic interest, but we can be pursued for much more than that.

When you discover that someone has been watching you to make you an offer of a relationship, a career or a promotion, it is a true honor. It's in these times where you see your value through someone else's eyes.

In 2 Chronicles 16, we learn about how King Asa is being rebuked for not looking to the Lord as his helper. The seer, Hanani, is speaking to King Asa about God's judgement against him, but in the midst of this judgement reveals something about the heart of God.

He says God is looking to and fro throughout the whole earth to find someone who is loyal to Him so that He might show Himself strong on their behalf.

This is our God, the One who is looking intently throughout the earth for us.

We get to experience the Presence, the favor and strength of the Lord because of God's search for us. We think we look for God, but He is looking to and fro for us.

Of course, He is looking for a heart that seeks Him as well. This is what the Presence is all about. When the eyes of the Lord seeking the earth meet the eyes of those who are loyal to Him, that is when we experience God.

He awakens the affections of our heart through His pursuit of relationship with us, and we respond by our loyalty of trusting in who He is and giving Him our hearts.

He meets us in this place.

What is God looking over the earth for?

A sold-out heart. God is looking for a people who are wholly devoted to Him.

This is a person of the Presence. One who wants God to be near no matter what it costs. Our ultimate allegiance and loyalty must be the Lord.

This is the fear of the Lord. This is the proper response to the pursuit of God over our lives, to be fully surrendered to Him.

Lord God, what love You have for me, that You are searching to and fro to find someone that loves You and is loyal to You above all others. Let holy fear be upon my life. I don't want You to search and look over me, but I want You to meet my gaze as one who is wholly devoted to You. I love You! In Jesus' name, amen.

Diligently Seek
August 10

But without faith it is impossible to please Him, for he who comes to God must believe that He is, and that He is a rewarder of those who diligently seek Him.
Hebrews 11:6 NKJV

Have you ever been so desperate for God that you ached for His Presence?

As of this writing, my wife and I finished leading a youth camp last week. Tonight, as I led a testimony time for the youth ministry at our church, a young lady talked about being so desperate for God. She shared about her desperation for God to meet with her in a real way at camp last week. You could feel her passion and sincerity for God.

She is more quiet and timid by nature, but she had a holy boldness upon her words as she told all the other young people that God met her in a real way.

She said to everyone that if they would seek God with all their heart, He would encounter them.

Oh, how my heart burns to see the youth of this generation passionately seeking an encounter with God.

God is looking for people that seek Him diligently.

Faith is how we please God, and we need to not only believe in Him, but believe that He rewards those who diligently seek His face.

God is looking for those who passionately pursue His heart and seek Him with diligence.

I've heard many Christians say that seeking God for some kind of reward is wrong and of a selfish motive. But Hebrews 6 makes it plain that God desires to reward us.

If we seek God for rewards for our own worldly pleasures, then we are in the wrong.

However, when the Presence is our reward, are we not to pursue Him with our whole heart?

In *The Pursuit of God*, A. W. Tozer said, "The man who has God for his treasure has all things in One." *

People of the Presence have God as their prize.

The reward of our faith is God Himself. He is the greatest treasure and reward. He is the longing of our souls. We need to be diligent in our pursuit of Him. He is longing to share Himself with us and reward us for seeking Him.

Do you see the desire of God's heart? He is not hidden from us in the sense that He wants us to miss Him. He is hidden to be found by those who seek Him and trust Him by faith.

He loves the heart that seeks after Him and is waiting to reward us.

Father God, I believe in You. I have faith in You. I want to touch Your heart and please You. You are a rewarder of those who diligently seek You. I shake off weariness and sluggishness. I choose to pursue You by Your grace. I have fixed my eyes upon You, and I will not relent until You reward me with Your Presence. In Jesus' name, amen.

The Radiance of God's Glory
August 11

In the past God spoke to our ancestors through the prophets at many times and in various ways, but in these last days he has spoken to us by his Son, whom he appointed heir of all things, and through whom also he made the universe. The Son is the radiance of God's glory and the exact representation of his being, sustaining all things by his powerful word. After he had provided purification for sins, he sat down at the right hand of the Majesty in heaven. So he became as much superior to the angels as the name he has inherited is superior to theirs.
Hebrews 1:1-4

What is the best way to get one of your friends to know what another friend looks like before they ever meet?

Well, I would say a picture.

As you might have heard the saying, a picture is worth a thousand words.

Pictures are so wonderful. My children love to pore over pictures and videos of their childhood for hours. I love the sound of them laughing and reminiscing about special memories.

Pictures can capture a moment in time that cements them in your mind.

The writer of Hebrews begins with this statement in verse one that God used to speak through the prophets. Then he adds a "but."

But in these last days he has spoken by His Son.

Who is the Son according to this passage?

Jesus, the Son of God, is the heir of all things, through whom the universe was made, the radiance of God's glory, the exact representation of His being, One who sustains all things by His powerful word, provided us purification of sins, sat down at the right hand of the Majesty in heaven and is superior to the angels.

Jesus is the picture of God.

He is the exact representation of His being.

The clearest picture we have of God is Jesus.

Jesus is how God speaks to us now. And Jesus is the radiance of God's glory.

Jesus is the Presence, God's radiating glory.

The Presence is in Him.

When we think of the Presence, our highest thoughts should be upon the Lord Jesus.

We associate angels with glory, and that is certainly fitting, but Jesus is superior to the angels. To go deeper in the Presence, what we really need is a greater revelation of Jesus.

We need to see Jesus.

Oh, how great is Jesus, who made the universe and upholds all things by the word of His power.

Yet He died for us to purify us from our sins.

There is no One like Jesus.

Going deeper in God's Presence is not about how we work it out, it's about loving Jesus and communing with Him.

He made the way for us, and He came to us so that the Presence was not something we had to achieve but Someone we receive.

As we receive who Jesus is we are invited deeper in the radiance of His glory.

Lord Jesus, I ache to see You. I have to have You. There is no one like You. You are better than the angels. You are the creator of the universe and You are all powerful. Yet You loved me enough to die for me. O, Son of God, the radiance of God's glory, reveal Yourself to me more and more. In Your name, amen.

The Alive and Active Word
August 12

For the word of God is alive and active. Sharper than any double-edged sword, it penetrates even to dividing soul and spirit, joints and marrow; it judges the thoughts and attitudes of the heart. Nothing in all creation is hidden from God's sight. Everything is uncovered and laid bare before the eyes of him to whom we must give account.
Hebrews 4:12-13

Do you read the Bible?
I once heard Bishop Jospeh Garlington say, "You don't read the Bible, the Bible reads you." *

The Bible is continually relevant.

It can speak to your current situation to bring conviction and encouragement, specifically when and how you need it.

The Bible is so powerful because it's the Word of God. It is a living Book and although ancient, the author is still alive to guide us and speak to us through His Word.

The writer of Hebrews says that the Word of God is alive and active.

It is sharper than a double-edged sword and can divide our soul and our spirit, our joints and marrow and judges the intent of our heart.

The Word of God tests and tries all of us and our motives. It is powerful and alive. It is like a surgeon's scalpel that can cut us to reveal us and to heal us.

The Word of God is like God's searchlight into the depths of our being. Nothing is hidden from God's sight. The Scripture lays our soul bare and uncovered before the eyes of the Lord to whom we will give an account.

The Bible brings us before the Presence of the Lord in a way that is without pretense or masks. The Word of God has the power to bring us before Him, not how we might want to pretend that we are, but how we truly are.

God truly loves us, but not in a way that powers a false pretense of who we are. He loves us unconditionally, but in His love, He longs to transform us and deliver us.

He can only deal with us in truth. His Word brings us into His Presence not only to feel His pleasure but also to expose us so He can change us to be more like Him.

The Word of God brings us into the Presence in our true condition by the power of His truth.

Lord, Your Word is living and active. It is powerful. I invite You to expose me and lay my soul bare before You. I want to truly encounter Your Presence, where I truly am in all of my faults and failures, so that Your powerful Word might deliver me and heal me. I love to come before Your eyes and be near You so that You can make me more like You. In Jesus' name, amen.

Approach with Confidence
August 13

Therefore, since we have a great high priest who has ascended into heaven, Jesus the Son of God, let us hold firmly to the faith we profess. For we do not have a high priest who is unable to empathize with our weaknesses, but we have one who has been tempted in every way, just as we are—yet he did not sin. Let us then approach God's throne of grace with confidence, so that we may receive mercy and find grace to help us in our time of need.
Hebrews 4:14-16

Have you ever been in trouble but then received mercy?

As a child, I got my fair share of discipline. One of the best feelings after getting caught for doing something wrong was when I received mercy.

Unexpected mercy is a life-changing experience.

We tend to be used to the idea that you do the crime; you pay the time.

But Jesus has something so much better for us.

Right after we read about how the Word of God reveals the intentions of our heart and we are laid bare without anything hidden before our Creator in Hebrews 4, we get a powerful "therefore".

One of the keys of Bible interpretation is to find out what a "therefore" is there for. Therefore is a connecting word.

"Therefore, since we have a great high priest..., Jesus the Son of God." The revealing and baring of our soul is connected to the truth that we have a high priest, Jesus Christ.

Jesus as our high priest is good news! This passage goes on to say that as our high priest, He empathizes with our weaknesses and is tempted in every way that we are, but without any sin. Jesus, through His love and compassion for us, has made a way for us into the Presence. He reveals where we have gone wrong so that we can repent and receive mercy to help us.

We can "approach God's throne of grace with confidence."

For what?

To "receive mercy and grace to help us in our time of need."

Our time of need does not disqualify us from the Presence.

If we come through Jesus, our high priest, we can approach God's throne with confidence in our time of need.

When we are needy, we usually feel least qualified.

But our qualification is not on our own merits.

We come on the merits of Christ and His great compassion for us. When you have a need and you come to God through Jesus, you have bold access to get mercy and grace.

We don't need to punish ourselves.

God doesn't reveal our sin, brokenness, pains, or needs to ever push us away.

He reveals our needs so we can boldly approach Him with confidence.

Lord Jesus, You are my perfect, sinless and compassionate High Priest. Thank You, that when You reveal my sin and my needs, it's to invite me into Your Presence to give me mercy and grace. You understand me because You were tempted just like me. You are the shame breaker and You have given me bold access to God's throne. I run to You in my needs. Thank You for Your love. In Jesus' name, amen.

A Better Offering
August 14

By faith Abel brought God a better offering than Cain did. By faith he was commended as righteous, when God spoke well of his offerings. And by faith Abel still speaks, even though he is dead.
Hebrews 11:4

Have you ever hosted someone for a meal and desired that they enjoy what you prepared?

I grew up in a home where my mom was such an excellent cook.

She put so much attention and detail into making sure that a meal was pulled off just right. She loved hosting people and giving them an experience with food that would please their heart.

It must be wired into our human nature that when we put effort into preparing food, we desire to hear about how much it pleases those we have prepared it for.

There is an offering that pleases the Lord and an offering that does not.

Hebrews 11, the hall of faith chapter in the Bible, is full of stories of those who pleased the Lord with their faith. Abel and his brother Cain were the first children in the Bible of Adam and Eve.

Abel brought an offering to the Lord of an animal sacrifice, and Cain's offering was from his work in the field.

We don't have specifics of what was wrong with Cain's offering and why Abel's was acceptable. But we do know that Abel brought the better offering.

Later, throughout the Torah, the first five books of the Bible, God accepted both animal and produce as acceptable sacrifices.

But what we learn in Hebrews 11 looking back at this story, is that Abel brought his offering to the Lord in faith. By faith, Abel was accepted as righteous and his life still speaks to us today.

We enter the Presence by bringing an offering to God in faith.

Abel is a picture of Jesus for us.

We become righteous by faith through the better sacrifice of Jesus.

We don't strive to get into the Presence. We come on God's terms like Abel.

God is not looking for our own efforts and for us to come on our own initiative like Cain.

Cain became jealous of Abel's worship and killed him over it.

When our worship is on our own terms, it reveals the anger and ugliness of our own heart. God is looking for pure and simple obedience to His desires, like Abel modeled for us.

We come before God to encounter Him through the better sacrifice of Jesus. We come by faith and come in light of the offering that is acceptable to God, the finished work of Christ.

Lord Jesus, I love You! I come to God through Your sacrifice. I approach You by faith, Lord, to make an offering of worship that blesses Your heart. I resist coming in my own striving and efforts. I renounce the selfish desires of the flesh to bring You worship on my own terms. You are worthy of true worship. I give You my heart. In Your name Jesus, amen.

Walked with God
August 15

By faith Enoch was taken from this life, so that he did not experience death: "He could not be found, because God had taken him away." For before he was taken, he was commended as one who pleased God.
Hebrews 11:5

Do you enjoy going on walks?

I love going on walks, especially with my wife. We have this beautiful walk not far from our home that goes by ponds and a river.

When I got sick before we were installed as senior pastors of our church, walking became a very important part of our lives.

Some people call it a superpower because of all the health benefits and the freedom from stress it produces.

I was so weak that walking a little further every day also helped me build confidence that I was getting stronger. I still love the time to walk and see the water and the mountains. It's good for the soul.

I also love how I am able to connect heart to heart with my wife as we walk and talk and pray together.

Enoch is in the hall of faith chapter in Hebrews. The Bible records very little about his life. He is mentioned in Genesis, Hebrews and Jude.

There is a book about his life that was popular literature during Jesus' day, but it was not canonized as Scripture. It is referenced by the Scripture, but the details we get about him basically boil down to the facts that Enoch pleased God by walking with God and God took him away supernaturally from this life to glory.

Genesis 5:24 says "And Enoch walked with God; and he was not, for God took him" (NKJV).

Then Hebrews commentary on his life was that he pleased God.

Again, we know there is more recorded about Enoch's life in his own book, but what God wanted us to know is so simple and powerful. The thing that pleased God the most about Enoch was that he was a man of the Presence. He walked with God.

The stories of Enoch in the *Book of Enoch* show that he is deeply spiritual and prophetic. He revealed great mysteries about spiritual warfare.

But God loved Enoch so much simply because he walked with Him.

There are only two people in the Bible who were spared by God supernaturally from death: Enoch and Elijah.

We know a lot about Elijah's exploits in Scripture, but what we know about Enoch is that his walk with God pleased God so much that he was walking with Him one moment in earth and the next he was walking with Him in the world to come.

His walk with God says that He spent time with God by sharing relationship and that He had a quality to His life that was holy.

Enoch shows us that a life wasted on being with God is not a waste at all.

The secret to those who touch God's heart is really not a secret at all. The ones who spend most of their life on God, walking with Him, please God the most and leave a major impact.

God, I want to walk with You like Enoch. I want to please You by spending my life with You. Forgive me, Lord, for being distracted by things that keep me busy but don't move Your heart. Let my life bring You pleasure. May I never lose the wonder that You simply want to spend time with me. The greatest things I can do are not for You, they are being with You. In Jesus' name, amen.

Off the Map
August 16

By faith Abraham, when called to go to a place he would later receive as his inheritance, obeyed and went, even though he did not know where he was going. By faith he made his home in the promised land like a stranger in a foreign country; he lived in tents, as did Isaac and Jacob, who were heirs with him of the same promise. For he was looking forward to the city with foundations, whose architect and builder is God.
Hebrews 11:8-10

Who is your go-to person for directions when you are driving?

One of the funny things about my wife is how confidently she answers questions about directions, even when she doesn't know which direction to go.

If I ask her, "What way do I turn?"

She will say so boldly, "Go right."

Then if I find out it's the wrong way and say, "This is the wrong way, why did you say to go this way?"

She replies, "Well, I don't know where to go. You asked me what way to turn, not if I knew where we were going."

Then we will just laugh and laugh as we continue on our journey.

What would you do if God called you to follow Him, and He didn't tell you where you were going?

Not just you, but your whole giant family with a bunch of your extended relatives?

Well, God told Abraham he was going to move, but he didn't know where. He was going to travel and live in tents.

But it didn't seem to matter to Abraham because he knew that God would be with him.

People have said, "Home is where the heart is."

I think for Abraham, home was where God is.

Abraham was looking forward to his eternal home, the eternal dwelling place that he would share with God. Somehow, he knew that following God now, even if it meant dwelling in a tent in the promised land, was connected to the ultimate promise of dwelling in the next life with God forever.

Those of the Presence are mostly concerned about dwelling with God in this life and the life to come.

It is costly to follow Jesus and obey God no matter what, but the reward is Him. There is no greater reward for following Jesus in this life than to know that you will dwell with God forever and ever.

Whatever we need to leave to follow God and have Him in our lives is of immeasurably greater worth than what we have left behind.

As Graham Cooke once shared a message on the life of Abraham, God still calls us to walk "off the map." *

Know this, whenever you follow Him and choose His Presence over the known and the familiar, He will be with You in this life and in the life to come, your greatest reward.

Father God, You are great. I will follow You. No matter what it cost, I want to follow Jesus. I yield the control of knowing the outcome of following Your Holy Spirit. I am a child of promise, and I look forward to the ultimate promise of dwelling in Your Presence forever in Your heavenly home. In Jesus' name, amen.

Seeing the Invisible
August 17

By faith Moses, when he had grown up, refused to be known as the son of Pharaoh's daughter. He chose to be mistreated along with the people of God rather than to enjoy the fleeting pleasures of sin. He regarded disgrace for the sake of Christ as of greater value than the treasures of Egypt, because he was looking ahead to his reward. By faith he left Egypt, not fearing the king's anger; he persevered because he saw him who is invisible.
Hebrews 11:24-27

Have you ever felt like more money would make you happier?
I remember hearing of an extremely wealthy man being asked what the one thing he would like was.
He said, "One more dollar."
How sad to have extreme wealth and to feel you never had enough. That's greed for you, though. Greed says you never have enough.
When I've traveled the world, it's amazing to meet people that are in poverty or at least don't have as much as we have in America, and are some of the happiest people I have ever met.

Poverty is not a blessing and if people have a certain level of need, it's horrible. But worldly treasures and pleasures of sin can keep us from the true riches of the Presence.

Moses is in the hall of faith in Hebrews 11 and the author of Hebrews lets us know that he chose suffering over the comforts and pleasures of being raised in Pharaoh's house. He was looking forward to identifying with Christ as greater than the treasure and wealth of Egypt.

Why could Moses forsake so much wealth and worldly pleasure?

Because He persevered, looking to Jesus and seeing Him who is invisible.

This is the cry of those of the Presence, "God I want to see You. Show me Your face Lord."

I read in an old book once of two saints. The first saint said, "I want to see the face of God."

The second saint said, "No can see the face of God and live."

To which the first replied, "Then let me see the face of God and die."

What Moses saw in the unseen was greater than all that could be seen with His natural eyes.

Seeing God changes everything.

I want to see His face.

The cry of every believer should be to get so close and be so near that you might behold His face. The secret to Moses' endurance and example of faith was seeing into the Presence.

In one sense, the Scripture says no one can see God and live, and on the other, it gives us examples of those who see Him.

We may not be able to fully see Him in this world the way we will in the next, but to whatever degree He reveals Himself, may seeing Him be our greatest reward.

Lord Jesus, I want to see You. I want to behold Your face. Your Presence, Your face and Your nearness is greater than all of the treasure and fame of this world. It would be greater to be disgraced in this world for You Christ Jesus than to have all the wealth of nations. You are my reward. In Your name, amen.

ANCIENT FUTURE FAITH
AUGUST 18

They were put to death by stoning; they were sawed in two; they were killed by the sword. They went about in sheepskins and goatskins, destitute, persecuted and mistreated— the world was not worthy of them. They wandered in deserts and mountains, living in caves and in holes in the ground. These were all commended for their faith, yet none of them received what had been promised, since God had planned something better for us so that only together with us would they be made perfect.
Hebrews 11:37-40

Do you have a hero of the faith?
    I grew up hearing stories about David Wilkerson and John Wimber in my house. My Dad was greatly impacted by the lives of these heroes of the faith.

I love reading about the lives and ministries of Saint Patrick, Jan Hus, John Wesley, William Seymour, Mother Basilea, Richard Wurmbrand, Reinhard Bonnke and Dr. Cho.

There are many men and women of God who cultivated a deep relationship with God in His Presence and impacted human history. Examples of faithful people who overcame great challenges or suffered for their beliefs strengthen our resolve to live boldly for God.

The hall of faith chapter closes in Hebrews 11 with not only a list of those who did great exploits and great miracles but also those who suffered greatly for Christ. Being a people of faith who diligently seek God, a people of the Presence, does not always guarantee us a life of ease and comfort.

In many ways, prioritizing Jesus and His Presence above everything will be a costly endeavor. Our confession that Jesus is worthy above all else, and our highest prize, will be tested in this life however God allows.

Don't judge someone's nearness to God or your own nearness to Him by the amount of prosperity or miracles that you see.

Those heroes of Hebrews 11 who saw great miracles, blessing and breakthrough, as well as those who suffered greatly for their faith, all had an incomplete promise. They were all waiting for Jesus and for the day that we live in now, where we can be saved by faith and the Spirit can live within us.

We are connected to the story of these heroes of faith. Their story is only fulfilled in us who continue to diligently seek God in our generation.

We have an ancient future faith. It's ancient because we look back to these who lived in the Presence throughout Biblical history and gain strength from their stories of how God was with them.

They were looking to the future by faith when and after Christ would come. They laid the foundation, and we are building upon it.

Find heroes of the faith that have gone before you that give you inspiration and strength to diligently seek the Presence.

―――

Lord Jesus, thank You so much for the heroes of faith that have gone before me. Thank You that I complete their faith. I am a part of the great story that You are writing as I diligently seek You. No matter if my story is full of blessing, suffering or some of both, may I live for Your glory. You are worthy! In Your name Jesus, amen.

The Author and Finisher
August 19

Therefore we also, since we are surrounded by so great a cloud of witnesses, let us lay aside every weight, and the sin which so easily ensnares us, and let us run with endurance the race that is set before us, looking unto Jesus, the author and finisher of our faith, who for the joy that was set before Him endured the cross, despising the shame, and has sat down at the right hand of the throne of God.
Hebrews 12:1-2 NKJV

Have you ever run in a race?

When I was in middle school I tried running on the track team for one year. I didn't really love running, but I thought I would try it out, anyway. I didn't have the greatest season, but I had some fun on the team.

My youth pastor, Russ Babcock, was a runner and a good track coach. He came to my last track meet of the year and gave me some pointers. I remember looking to him as I ran.

Having his support, encouragement and his wisdom helped me have the best performance of the whole season.

The Christian life is all about having our eyes upon the right coach and the right source: Jesus Christ. The hall of faith chapter is followed by the reminder that we are surrounded by these heroes who have gone before us, cheering us on as we continue the race of faith they once began.

But our ultimate focus is not upon their example, but who their example pointed to: Jesus, the author and finisher of our faith.

We see here that life is likened to a race for which we need endurance. So, we have to lay aside every weight and sin that easily ensnares us. It's easy to get distracted, discouraged and weighed down by sin.

But as we keep our eyes on Jesus, we endure and overcome.

This is what it means to live in the Presence: to be all about Jesus.

He is our author and finisher.

He is the source of our strength.

He endured the cross, despised the shame of it, and sat down victorious at the right hand of God's throne.

He did it for the joy set before Him. We are the joy of Jesus.

We are His joy and prize.

He is our joy and prize.

Through the cross, the complete work, Jesus authors and finishes our faith. We live in the Presence as we set our gaze upon Him who welcomed us in, sustains us and carries us to the finish line.

Let this entire race of life and pursuit of the Presence begin, continue and end with your eyes upon the One who gave it all for you, His joy.

Precious Jesus, You are the author and finisher of my faith. I set my eyes upon You. I cast off every weight and sin that easily ensnares me to run this race. Thank You for the cross. I enter into and delight in Your joy over me. There is no one like You. I exalt You! In Your name, amen.

LEGITIMATE SONS
AUGUST 20

If you endure chastening, God deals with you as with sons; for what son is there whom a father does not chasten? But if you are without chastening, of which all have become partakers, then you are illegitimate and not sons. Furthermore, we have had human fathers who corrected us, and we paid them respect. Shall we not much more readily be in subjection to the Father of spirits and live? For they indeed for a few days chastened us as seemed best to them, but He for our profit, that we may be partakers of His holiness. Now no chastening seems to be joyful for the present, but painful; nevertheless, afterward it yields the peaceable fruit of righteousness to those who have been trained by it.
Hebrews 12:7-11 NKJV

How did you get disciplined growing up?

I got time outs in my room. I hated being sent to my room.

I also got swats, and I didn't like those either.

Sometimes I would get those speeches from my parents like "This hurts me more than it hurts you," or, "I really wish I didn't have to do this."

I would think, "Then why do this?"

While I did not enjoy being disciplined, I knew my parents loved me and corrected me so I would learn to live right and deal with my negative behaviors.

God's nearness is not all sunshine and rainbows.

God's nearness will certainly bring His favor and love, but His love and favor does not always manifest as the things we enjoy.

Sometimes, God's nearness brings His discipline in love. God's discipline affirms His love for us and our identity of sonship.

Being a person of the Presence means welcoming His discipline in our lives.

Isn't it amazing to know we don't have to be afraid of God's discipline?

Rather, we can welcome His discipline knowing it's His affirmation that we are loved.

His discipline and chastening in our life produces holiness in us. It can be painful, but it's for our profit. We learn to abide in the Presence through His discipline because we experience "the peaceable fruit of righteousness."

This is Presence language.

If we are not disciplined, we are not children of God.

If we are disciplined, we are legitimate sons.

I always knew my parents loved me and I wasn't afraid of them. However, I had a reverential fear of doing things that would hurt them in front of them.

Being open to God's Presence brings us a holy fear, knowing that His discipline proves His love for us and shapes us to be like Him.

Father God, thank You for Your love for me. I receive Your love not only how I like it, but also through Your discipline. I fear You. Search my heart and life. I welcome Your correction and chastening so that I might know my identity as a legitimate son. I love You. In Jesus' name, amen.

Without Holiness
August 21

Pursue peace with all people, and holiness, without which no one will see the Lord:
Hebrews 12:14 NKJV

Have you ever been denied entry somewhere because you were wearing the wrong clothes?

When I was a little boy, probably around three or four years old, my parents got blessed with a vacation to an upscale resort. We went to the restaurant at the resort for dinner one night and they wouldn't let my dad in to eat.

Why?

Because he was not wearing a blazer. He had to have a suit coat on and so they gave him one that totally clashed with his shorts and t-shirt.

At least we got into the place. It was a little embarrassing, but there was no getting a table without the right clothes.

There is no getting to see Jesus without holiness. Holiness is not optional for Christians. This is why we must welcome His discipline. We need Him to correct us in His love so that we might be holy.

If we want to be a person that gets near enough to see Him in the Presence, we must realize that holiness is not optional.

Some people interpret this Scripture more metaphorically, that you can't see Jesus or have a close relationship with Him if you don't live a holy life.

Others see it more literally, like you can never get to see Jesus in heaven if you don't live a holy life.

The Eastern Orthodox believe that the soul goes on a spiritual journey after death and is continually purified until holy enough to see Jesus.

The Roman Catholics believe in purgatory, where those who are believers but not yet holy go to continually be purified enough to see Jesus.

While I don't hold to either of these positions, I respect that they take the idea of being holy as a serious prerequisite to see Jesus.

We must live a holy life to see Jesus. We should take this literally.

To be holy is to be set apart. The way we live matters. It's not just our confession of faith, but the living out of our faith that matters to the Lord.

If we want to sustain a life in the Presence here and now, we must continue in holiness. To see Him on that day at the end, we must continue in holiness.

Our holiness comes through the blood of Jesus. This is not about sinless perfection, but a pursuit of holiness by the grace that Christ has given us.

If seeing Jesus is the greatest gift and holiness is the way to see Him, then we ought not see this as only an obligation, but also an invitation.

Lord Jesus, thank You for the way into Your Presence by Your blood. I love You Lord. I want to see You. I welcome Your search, Your conviction and Your discipline that I may endure in holiness. Deliver me and cleanse me from sin, mixture and uncleanness that I may be set apart unto You. In Your holy name, amen.

Consuming Fire
August 22

For if they did not escape who refused Him who spoke on earth, much more shall we not escape if we turn away from Him who speaks from heaven, whose voice then shook the earth; but now He has promised, saying, "Yet once more I shake not only the earth, but also heaven." Now this, "Yet once more," indicates the removal of those things that are being shaken, as of things that are made, that the things which cannot be shaken may remain. Therefore, since we are receiving a kingdom which cannot be shaken, let us have grace, by which we may serve God acceptably with reverence and godly fear. For our God is a consuming fire.
Hebrews 12:25-29 NKJV

Have you ever been near a raging fire?

In high school I took a special class on firefighting. We got to use fire trucks, ladders, oxygen tanks and high power hoses to train and prepare for a career in firefighting.

I ended up on a different career path, but I enjoyed the experience. At the end of the year, we went to fight live fire in a controlled environment at the state fire academy. We went up floors in a concrete tower and different rooms had fires lit by the academy staff.

I remember pulling off my glove in the room with smoke pouring everywhere and I could barely lift my hand off the ground because of the pain I felt from the intense heat.

Everyone respects fire. Fire is hot, smokey and can be destructive.

As the book of Hebrews is coming to an end, the author reminds us that Jesus is the fulfillment of all that was spoken to Israel. As God spoke and shook the earth in Exodus, so God says He will once again shake the earth and heaven. He will shake everything in this world so that what can't be shaken is all that is left. What remains is built only on the true foundation: the unshakable kingdom of God.

In God's Kingdom, we have received the grace of God, which causes us to live in reverence and the fear of the Lord.

Why is all this true?

Because God is a consuming fire.

When we come into the Presence, we must respect the One who is a consuming fire. We approach the Presence with reverence. There is a way that we approach our holy God, who shakes all things. There is a way we approach the One who gives us grace so undeserving.

The way we approach Him is in godly fear.

I see some people so flippant and casual in worship.

If you are flippant and casual with fire, that is how you get burned.

Fire gives us warmth, light and energy.

Fire is wonderful.

Fire is a blessing.

But when fire is not reverenced, it can be to your own hurt.

Reverence the God who consumes all things.

The Presence is full of fire.

O God, You are a consuming fire. I reverence You because of Your great power and Your great grace. There is no one like You who speaks and shakes the earth and the heavens. Let my life be built on Your true Kingdom foundation. Let me live in godly fear and approach You with awe and respect. In Jesus' name, amen.

The Highway of Holiness
August 23

The parched ground shall become a pool, And the thirsty land springs of water; In the habitation of jackals, where each lay, There shall be grass with reeds and rushes. A highway shall be there, and a road, And it shall be called the Highway of Holiness. The unclean shall not pass over it, But it shall be for others. Whoever walks the road, although a fool, Shall not go astray. No lion shall be there, Nor shall any ravenous beast go up on it; It shall not be found there. But the redeemed shall walk there, And the ransomed of the Lord shall return, And come to Zion with singing, With everlasting joy on their heads. They shall obtain joy and gladness, And sorrow and sighing shall flee away.
Isaiah 35:7-10 NKJV

What is your favorite highway or road to drive on?

My two favorite places to drive are on the river road near my house and on the highways of southern Utah.

I love the river road because it's close to home. It gently

winds back and forth by the Snohomish river surrounded by farmland and beautiful views of the valley and mountains.

The highways of southern Utah are wide open roads with a high speed limit and an almost endless view of painted desert cliffs and hills.

The Lord has a highway for us. I think it's His favorite. It's called the *Highway of Holiness.*

In Isaiah 35, God is speaking of the great turnaround He will bring to His people. The parched ground and desert will become a pool and a land of water springs.

In this supernatural desert becoming a place of water and growth, there is a Highway of Holiness for those who give up uncleanness. This highway is a place of protection from all predators. It's a place of singing and rejoicing with everlasting joy.

How do we get on this highway?

Through the gospel.

That's how we receive entrance on this great road.

Who walks this road?

Those who are "although fools, shall not go astray."

We may be fools, but we are God's fools.

When my dad was in college, there was a street preacher who was mocked and ridiculed. He wore a sandwich board sign over his shoulders and preached the gospel.

The front said, "I'm a fool for Jesus."

The back said, "Whose fool are you?"

We are all a fool for something.

Those who are unashamed to be a fool for Jesus and sold out to the pursuit of the Presence are the "redeemed" and the "ransomed of the Lord."

We are the ones who are so overcome with everlasting joy that we can only sing and praise as "sorrow and sighing shall flee away."

Jesus, I will be a fool for You if it means that I have Your Presence. You are worthy of my whole life. Thank You for the Highway of Holiness. I rejoice in You, for You have redeemed me and ransomed me. I love Your Presence. I rejoice with everlasting joy and sing to You, my Lord. In Your name, amen.

THOSE WHO WAIT
AUGUST 24

Have you not known? Have you not heard? The everlasting God, the Lord, The Creator of the ends of the earth, Neither faints nor is weary. His understanding is unsearchable. He gives power to the weak, And to those who have no might He increases strength. Even the youths shall faint and be weary, And the young men shall utterly fall, But those who wait on the Lord Shall renew their strength; They shall mount up with wings like eagles, They shall run and not be weary, They shall walk and not faint.
Isaiah 40:28-31 NKJV

What was the hardest thing to wait for growing up?

I think the hardest thing for me was waiting to open presents on Christmas Day. It's not like I had to wait all day. But I could barely sleep on Christmas Eve because I was so excited for the next day.

I always woke up early on Christmas morning and had to wait for my parents to wake up. We had to wait to read the Bible story of Jesus' birth and sing Happy Birthday to Jesus before we could open our stockings, and then the first presents.

It really wasn't that long, but it felt like forever as we waited each year.

Isaiah 40:31 is one of those promises of Scripture that is like a crown jewel of all Scriptures, a beautiful and reviving truth for all those who have grown weary. The context is that God never tires or faints. He gives power to the weak, and He increases our strength. Oh, how great is the Presence of the Lord that we might receive power when we are worn down and tired.

How do we receive this strength and power in our lives?

We wait.

Specifically, we wait on the Lord.

"Wait" is also translated as "hope."

This waiting on the Lord is about abiding in His Presence.

It's about anticipating His goodness and His strength.

Waiting is not inactivity in a sense that we totally disconnect. Oh yes, we must disconnect from stress and striving. But waiting is an active hope and attention on the Lord to commune with Him and receive from Him.

When we wait on the Lord, we are like those who mount up with wings like eagles. In the Presence, as we wait on Him, He turns the winds of adversity that have wearied us into opportunities for us to soar higher like the eagles do.

We can become so strong from waiting on the Lord that we run and won't grow weary, we walk and do not faint.

What are you waiting for?

Hurry up and wait!

Lord God, the everlasting One, the Creator of all, who is never tired or weary, I come to Your Presence to wait upon You. My hope is in You. When I am weak and tired, You renew me and strengthen me. I will soar like the eagles. In You I run and won't grow weary, I walk and won't faint. Help me to continue to wait upon You. In Jesus' name, amen.

The Awakened Ear
August 25

The Lord God has given Me The tongue of the learned, That I should know how to speak A word in season to him who is weary. He awakens Me morning by morning, He awakens My ear To hear as the learned. The Lord God has opened My ear; And I was not rebellious, Nor did I turn away. I gave My back to those who struck Me, And My cheeks to those who plucked out the beard; I did not hide My face from shame and spitting. "For the Lord God will help Me; Therefore I will not be disgraced; Therefore I have set My face like a flint, And I know that I will not be ashamed. He is near who justifies Me; Who will contend with Me? Let us stand together. Who is My adversary? Let him come near Me. Surely the Lord God will help Me; Who is he who will condemn Me? Indeed they will all grow old like a garment; The moth will eat them up.
Isaiah 50:4-9 NKJV

Have you ever met someone who seemed to have a secret to their success?

Some influencers, authors and successful entrepreneurs say their success is all about their daily routine. They typically claim that the morning is the most important part of the day.

This is the time to be quiet before the day gets busy and interrupted. High performers often fill their mornings with a time to read, practice their faith, exercise and handle what they think is the most important business priority.

Jesus is, in some sense, the greatest influencer of all time (of course, to describe Him as an influencer is just a minuscule example of His greatness). Long before it was popular to have a morning routine, Jesus spent time in the Presence during the first part of His day.

Isaiah 50 is one of what are referred to as the four *Servant Songs* of Isaiah.

It is a prophetic passage about Jesus. This prophecy references the daily routine of Jesus.

Jesus' daily routine was for the Father to awaken His ear morning by morning, to hear as the learned.

This is how Jesus always knew what to say. His voice could awaken the lost, the hurting and the dead because His ear was awakened.

Jesus lived by the word that God the Father spoke to Him. "He set His face like flint" to even die on the cross.

He lived and died by the word spoken to Him. This passage says that by what He heard, He was not shamed, disgraced, ashamed, contended against or condemned.

Jesus was with the Father daily to hear His voice. He responded by obeying His father.

If we are to have success in our calling, purpose or ministry, we need to practice the Presence daily and treasure hearing His voice above all else. Jesus' awakened ear led Him to suffer so we could enter God's glory.

May our ears be awakened to hear that we might obey and awaken those with the word of the Lord.

Lord Jesus, I am moved by Your example of suffering. Although You suffered humiliation and pain, You were free from shame, condemnation and disgrace because You lived by the voice of the Father. Help me to hear His voice like You. Give me an awakened ear to obey, so I might have a voice that awakens the dead. In Your glorious name, amen.

While He May Be Found

August 26

Seek the Lord while He may be found, Call upon Him while He is near. Let the wicked forsake his way, And the unrighteous man his thoughts; Let him return to the Lord, And He will have mercy on him; And to our God, For He will abundantly pardon.
Isaiah 55:6-7 NKJV

Have you ever felt pressure to make a decision on a short deadline?

Making a big decision can be really stressful.

Someone who has been a teacher and support to me in ministry, Dr. Wayde Goodall, once told me, "When I feel pushed towards something, it is usually my flesh. When I feel drawn towards something, it is usually the Lord."

We shouldn't feel pressured to make decisions, but we also can't be passive either. Some opportunities will fade away or vanish altogether.

On one extreme, we have to avoid being rushed, but on the other, we have to avoid what some call "analysis paralysis."

Over analyzing and delaying obedience can really be disobedience and a chance to miss out on what God has for us.

In Isaiah 55, Isaiah is preaching to the people, "Seek the Lord while He may be found, call upon Him while He is near."

Do you hear the passion in His voice?

Don't miss your moment!

When God is near, when you sense the Presence, that is when you call upon Him and seek Him.

Leonard Ravenhill once said, "The opportunity of a lifetime must be seized in the lifetime of the opportunity." *

How many times are people in worship when God's Presence manifests and there is a call to the altar but no response?

How many times have I had a chance to spend time in prayer and be alone with God and I get distracted by my to-do list or even worse by my phone?

How many chances does God graciously give us to respond to His nearness even when we fail to respond?

The best time to seek God is now.

You don't have tomorrow guaranteed.

The best time to respond, surrender and obey is now. The Lord is looking for us to fully return to Him and His desire is to show us mercy and abundantly pardon us for our sins.

But we must come when we have the chance.

I have never regretted following Jesus. My only regrets are when I didn't obey and take the opportunity to be with Him or do what He told me to do the first time.

Every time, His nearness is an invitation to seek Him and find Him, an opportunity to call upon Him and receive mercy.

What we need is in His Presence and He will keep coming, but will you respond while you have the chance?

Lord, I love Your Presence. Your nearness to me is my greatest delight. Deliver me from passivity. I choose to seek You, God of mercy. I call upon You when You are near. I renounce delays and distractions. I return to You. I run to You. I give You the first and the best part of me with quick obedience. In Jesus' name, amen.

The Chosen Fast
August 27

Is it a fast that I have chosen, A day for a man to afflict his soul? Is it to bow down his head like a bulrush, And to spread out sackcloth and ashes? Would you call this a fast, And an acceptable day to the Lord? "Is this not the fast that I have chosen: To loose the bonds of wickedness, To undo the heavy burdens, To let the oppressed go free, And that you break every yoke? Is it not to share your bread with the hungry, And that you bring to your house the poor who are cast out; When you see the naked, that you cover him, And not hide yourself from your own flesh? Then your light shall break forth like the morning, Your healing shall spring forth speedily, And your righteousness shall go before you; The glory of the Lord shall be your rear guard.
Isaiah 58:5-8 NKJV

Have you ever fasted from food?

Fasting is a powerful discipline.

I have learned a lot about fasting in the past several years.

When I was really sick, I learned about the power of fasting to heal the body when it receives a break. Fasting not only yields physical benefits but also incredible spiritual benefits.

Fasting doesn't change God's mind when we pray, but it positions us in a place of weakness, humility, and dependency to more fully rely on God's power.

The Lord lets us know in Isaiah 58 that He has a chosen fast for us. He tells His people, Israel that fasting should be a time of humility and afflicting our own soul. Fasting with the right heart posture releases God's freedom over us from oppression. God's chosen fast releases breakthrough over our lives.

Our fasting should also be accompanied by agreeing with God's freedom, feeding the hungry and clothing the naked.

God is not looking for a spiritual piety that is divorced from righteous and just actions. We can act very spiritual in prayer, but God is looking for true spirituality that affects those around us as well.

When we fast with humility and seek God while we also obey Him by caring for those who are suffering, God grants us incredible promises, "Our light will break forth like the morning, your healing spring forth speedily... and the glory of the Lord will be your rear guard."

The Presence is promised for our protection when we seek God like this!

In a recent baptism, a young lady testified at our church that she and her husband (boyfriend at the time) came to our church for about a year and didn't really feel anything sinking in. Then they decided to spend some time in prayer and fasting at the beginning of the year with us, and everything started changing in their relationship with God. Every month, there has been some new breakthrough in their walk with God.

Fasting God's way releases blessing and breakthrough in our lives.

Lord God, help me to fast and pray. May I fast with godly mourning and acts of righteousness and justice. Teach me Your ways that lead to freedom and breakthrough for myself, my family and my nation. Let Your healing spring forth and may Your glory be my rear guard. In Jesus' name, amen.

Arise and Shine
August 28

Arise, shine; For your light has come! And the glory of the Lord is risen upon you. For behold, the darkness shall cover the earth, And deep darkness the people; But the Lord will arise over you, And His glory will be seen upon you. The Gentiles shall come to your light, And kings to the brightness of your rising. "Lift up your eyes all around, and see: They all gather together, they come to you; Your sons shall come from afar, And your daughters shall be nursed at your side. Then you shall see and become radiant, And your heart shall swell with joy; Because the abundance of the sea shall be turned to you, The wealth of the Gentiles shall come to you.
Isaiah 60:1-5 NKJV

Did you enjoy watching game shows as a kid?

I loved watching game shows when I was young. I would dream about winning vacations, cars, motor homes and, of course, a lot of money.

My favorite game show was *The Price is Right*. The excitement about that show was you didn't know who from the audience was going to be selected as the next contestant. When the call came, the camera panned back and forth frantically looking for who the happy contestant was. When someone's name was called, they would hug, high five, smile, scream and jump up and down.

We have a greater reason to rejoice and scream. God has called our name, and it's our time to arise and shine.

Some scholars believe this promise is only for the Millennial reign of Jesus, others see it as a picture of the church now because of Christ. I believe there is an initial fulfillment in the church now and a greater fulfillment in the world to come.

What a promise that the glory of the Lord has risen upon us!

When darkness covers the nation, The Lord arises over us and His glory will be seen upon us! In times of darkness and chaos in the world, those of the Presence stand out even more. The nations will come to our light because of Christ shining upon us. We "become radiant" and our hearts swell with joy as the abundance of the nation turns towards us. Who we behold in the Presence causes our faces to shine and the nations of the earth to join us.

I've heard many preachers say we become what we behold.

Time in the Presence gives us a countenance that is radiant, because the glory of God has an effect upon us. We become radiant in the Presence of God, and that radiance becomes a contrasting witness to the world around us.

This is the missional aspect to the Presence. When we arise and shine, not only do we glorify God, we draw the lost and hurting to Him as we reflect His glory to all people.

Lord Jesus, I have beheld You and I am radiant with Your Presence. Let Your glory increase upon my life. I hear Your voice to arise and shine. I am not ashamed to reflect Your glory to the nations. How my heart swells with joy at Your Presence. Let others turn to You as Your glory rests upon me. In Your name, amen.

Two Sins
August 29

My people have committed two sins: They have forsaken me, the spring of living water, and have dug their own cisterns, broken cisterns that cannot hold water.
Jeremiah 2:13

Do you think we are all worshippers?

I've heard many preachers over the years talk about how we are all worshippers of something. I have to agree with this statement. We try to find meaning in our lives, whether we are Christians, spiritual, religious or even non-religious.

Our culture is filled with pleasure seeking through sports stadiums, rock concerts, festivals, fame, wealth, power and notoriety. Every one of us finds something to worship in our lives that is bigger than us and gives us purpose and some kind of satisfaction.

Jeremiah is prophesying judgement against God's people Israel and charging them with committing two sins.

The first sin is that they had forsaken God, "the spring of living water."

The second sin they committed was that they dug their own cisterns which were broken and could not hold water.

This first sin is truly the sin of sins. This first sin of forsaking God is what ultimately leads to our destruction. God Himself is our salvation. Jesus made this clear in His claims that He is the source of life, of living water. When we withdraw from the Presence and forsake Him, we are forsaking our only source of life and refreshing.

This second sin of digging our own cisterns that can't hold water reveals that we can be so foolish and that we are all worshippers.

Cisterns are tanks or reservoirs that hold water. So not only do we forsake God as the spring of living water, we create our own containers for holding water that can't hold water.

This reveals that we are all seeking the Presence, but when we turn from the true source, we create a counterfeit presence in our lives that cannot satisfy or cannot hold water.

Fidelity to Jesus as our only source of the Presence is for our own pleasure. Turning from Him and trying to create our own pleasure and satisfaction through other worship leaves us empty and dry.

Don't be tempted to turn from Him. There is no life, power, and true satisfaction outside of Him and what His hand provides.

Lord Jesus, You are my Source of living water, a spring that never runs dry. Let me never turn from Your Presence in my life. I give You my worship. Cleanse my life from any idols, from any cisterns that I have attempted to turn to instead of You. Be my all in all. I am satisfied in You alone. In Jesus' name, amen.

WHOLEHEARTEDNESS
AUGUST 30

You will seek me and find me when you seek me with all your heart.
Jeremiah 29:13

If you have children, what do you look for in encouraging them in a good direction in their life?

In one word, I think we look for wholeheartedness.

Grace and I are blessed with four amazing children.

Sometimes, they'll start something—a sport, hobby, or course of study—and quickly lose interest.

But occasionally my children get involved in something to which they give their whole heart. Where it's frustrating to motivate an unmotivated child, it's an incredibly rewarding feeling to watch them pursue something with all they've got.

God is also looking for wholeheartedness.

Leanord Ravenhill once said, "The only reason we don't have revival is because we can live without it." *

I think this is true of God's manifest Presence in our lives. The only reason we don't have the Presence is because we can live without it.

In Jeremiah 29, God is telling His people that after they are exiled for 70 years, He has not cast them off to destroy them forever. He gives them a promise in the midst of His judgement against them.

The famous verse people love to quote, Jeremiah 29:11 says, "For I know the plans I have for you," declares the Lord, "plans to prosper you and not to harm you, plans to give you hope and a future."

This seems to be a feel-good verse for us as individuals, but it's actually a covenant promise to be remembered by God's people during chastisement.

Then God says to His people that since He promised them good when they pray (v. 12), He will allow Himself to be found when they seek Him with all of their heart.

This promise has a condition.

God tells us how He treats His people, but He is looking for a prayerful people who are wholehearted in going after Him.

I've seen so many Christians who pray for the Holy Spirit baptism for a few minutes, and if they don't speak in tongues right away, resign that it's not God's will for their life.

I see Christians who are facing great odds or crisis, yet they devote little time to prayer and seeking God.

I hear believers describe the great things they want to see God do in their lives, but there is so little motivation to attend a prayer meeting.

Where is the wholeheartedness?

Where is the seeking God until you find Him?

Seeking God is not about self-effort and self-motivation, it's about a revelation of invitation from our Almighty Creator. He wants to see us respond in the maturity of our desire for Him.

Don't go half-heartedly after the Presence. Give yourself fully to the pursuit of God and you will find Him.

Lord God, I seek You with my whole heart. I give up lukewarm living and half-hearted pursuit of Your Presence. Reveal the power of Your invitation and promise in my life. I'm coming after You with all that I am. I love You above all others. In Jesus' name, amen.

Wasted Dwelling
August 31

He has laid waste his dwelling like a garden; he has destroyed his place of meeting. The Lord has made Zion forget her appointed festivals and her Sabbaths; in his fierce anger he has spurned both king and priest. The Lord has rejected his altar and abandoned his sanctuary. He has given the walls of her palaces into the hands of the enemy; they have raised a shout in the house of the Lord as on the day of an appointed festival.
Lamentations 2:6-7

Is there anything worse than a loss in sports to your greatest rival? There was a saying by Jim McKay on ABC's the *Wide World of Sports* that captured the intensity of emotion in competition: "The thrill of victory and the agony of defeat."

Victory is so sweet, which makes defeat so devastating.

I had a sports literature class in college. My teacher said he believed that each Monday in America you could tell if a city's NFL team won the day before by the general attitude of people around town. He thought there was something about professional American football that could really affect the morale of a community.

Losing, and especially losing to a team that you despise the most, can feel like a violation.

Lamentations is a short book by Jeremiah. It's a collection of poetry lamenting or mourning God's judgement of destruction over Jerusalem.

In Lamentations 2, Jeremiah describes the loss, destruction and waste as ultimately attributed to the Presence leaving Zion and the temple. "God laid waste His dwelling... Destroyed His place of meeting, rejected His altar and abandoned His sanctuary."

Ultimately, He "made Zion forget her festivals... and given the enemy... a shout" in the same day the festival was appointed.

The very place that was for the Presence of God Himself to dwell, He forsook.

On top of that, the place to celebrate God was given to their rival, their enemy, to shout and celebrate over them.

We need to grieve the loss of His Presence in our lives.

If God didn't show up in our church, would we notice it?

If God forsakes dwelling with us, meeting with us and being at our altars or in our sanctuary, would it grieve us?

The greatest judgment is the loss of God being with us.

Our nation is God-forsaken because God rejects our altars.

This should move us to tears and repentance.

His Presence is not optional.

If God abandons being with us, then the enemy gets a place in our lives.

God's Presence is what brings His blessing and protection.

May we attract Him with the posture of our hearts to honor Him and host His Presence. If He leaves, may we be humble, broken and desperate that He would return to the place of meeting with us.

Lord, if You are not present, I don't want to go through the motions of church and religion. Our culture and nation feel so God-forsaken. I know that only Your Presence makes the difference. In my life, my church and my nation, I pray that You would dwell with us, meet with us, return to the altar, return to the sanctuary and drive the enemy from us, that we might celebrate Your goodness. In Jesus' name, amen.

It is Good to Wait
September 1

I say to myself, "The Lord is my portion; therefore I will wait for him." The Lord is good to those whose hope is in him, to the one who seeks him; it is good to wait quietly for the salvation of the Lord... For no one is cast off by the Lord forever. Though he brings grief, he will show compassion, so great is his unfailing love.
Lamentations 3:24-26, 31-32

How would rate your joy in waiting?

I am not great at waiting by nature. I like to take action and get things done.

Growing up, I hated waiting for my mom and my sister to get ready. Of course, guys have it easier when it comes to getting ready for an event.

I remember sitting with my dad and my brother in our car moaning and saying, "Dad, when are they going to get out here? Can we just go without them?"

But going without them was not an option. The only option we had was to wait.

In Lamentations, this short book is mostly full of mourning the judgement and devastation that God released over disobedient Israel. But in chapter 3, Jeremiah says "The Lord is my portion, there I will wait for Him."

He goes on to say the Lord is good to those who hope in Him and it is good to wait for the Lord's salvation.

Hope has broken through in the midst of despair.

Why does hope come to Jeremiah in judgement?

Sometimes when all is lost we get clarity in these times.

Hope arises because the truth comes into focus as Jeremiah says, "No one is cast off by the Lord forever."

He says God brings us grief, but He will show compassion in His unfailing love.

When you have lost the Presence and all the blessings that come from Him, the only hope we have is to return to Him and wait. Going without Him is not an option.

Rebuilding on your own is not an option.

He is our only hope. We can't go without Him, so we wait for Him and we wait upon Him.

It is good to wait for the Lord.

Go all in on God.

Sometimes we are tempted to rebuild in our own strength and take matters into our own hands, but what we often need is a greater waiting and a deeper surrender.

For the Lord is our portion and only He can satisfy.

He is worth the wait.

Lord God, I wait upon You. Who can I run to? How can I fix my own mess? It is good to wait upon You, O Lord, my portion. I seek You and wait upon You for Your salvation. Your love for me is unfailing. Teach my heart to be patient and wait upon You. In Jesus' name, amen.

Fire and Glory

September 2

Above the vault over their heads was what looked like a throne of lapis lazuli, and high above on the throne was a figure like that of a man. I saw that from what appeared to be his waist up he looked like glowing metal, as if full of fire, and that from there down he looked like fire; and brilliant light surrounded him. Like the appearance of a rainbow in the clouds on a rainy day, so was the radiance around him. This was the appearance of the likeness of the glory of the Lord. When I saw it, I fell facedown, and I heard the voice of one speaking.
Ezekiel 1:26-28

Have you ever seen superhero movies or comic books? Superhero movies and comic books tap into our desire for supernatural beings and powers. Each character in these stories has special powers, and it seems like each new character becomes more powerful than the last.

As a youth, my mind was captivated by superheroes who could fly, travel through space, destroy planets, and protect against evil. These heroes had glorious features that made them superhuman. They were awesome and impressive.

When we think of the Presence, there is a space for being calm and peaceful with God, but there is also a fire and glory to His person and nature.

When we behold the Lord, and His Presence manifests, we should see Him as One who is like "glowing metal... full of fire...brilliant light surrounded...rainbow in the clouds...radiance...the likeness of the glory of the Lord."

We should live in holy awe of the Presence.

When was the last time you were awestruck by an encounter with the Lord?

We ought not to be so causal before Him.

We should tread with a holy fear and be impressed by His awesome power and might.

Oh, that we would be captivated by His radiance.

Sometimes people explain their encounters with the Lord like He is a big teddy bear or their buddy next door. I think to know God's tender love and mercy, His gentleness and kindness, is important, but it's even more powerful when we realize how gentle He is while being so awesome and powerful.

All superheroes pale in comparison to His greatness.

May we fall before Him as Ezekiel did when He saw Him.

Lord, I want to see You like Ezekiel did. Open my eyes to behold Your glory and fire. Let me see Your radiance. Come near, so near until I fall facedown at the brightness of Your shining. Captivate my heart with holy fear and the awesome wonder of who You are. In Jesus' name, amen.

Recapture

September 3

Therefore speak to them and tell them, 'This is what the Sovereign Lord says: When any of the Israelites set up idols in their hearts and put a wicked stumbling block before their faces and then go to a prophet, I the Lord will answer them myself in keeping with their great idolatry. I will do this to recapture the hearts of the people of Israel, who have all deserted me for their idols...' Then the people of Israel will no longer stray from me, nor will they defile themselves anymore with all their sins. They will be my people, and I will be their God, declares the Sovereign Lord.'
Ezekiel 14:4-5, 11

Have you ever lost your way with God?

I remember a season as a young man, where someone who was in grief shared out of his pain and it really affected me. I started to doubt God's desire to heal and felt my faith waning.

I went to a church service where Bill Johnson taught about the church being Bethel, or house of God, from the life of Jacob. In a moment, the idols of my heart were exposed and removed.

God recaptured my heart.

Looking back, what that young man shared with me didn't cause me to doubt God as much as it gave me an excuse to doubt Him.

In Ezekiel, God is saying to His people that when we set up idols in our hearts, He will allow prophets in our lives who will confirm our idols.

This is a rather sobering reality.

We can't trust our experiences.

There is a false presence that we can enter into. The crazy thing is that God will allow this to expose the powerlessness of our idols.

His main purpose is to recapture us. Then we "no longer stray" and we don't defile ourselves in our sins. Ultimately, we become a people once again of the true Presence where we are His people, and He is our God.

Is there anything greater than us being His people and He being our God?

This is what we have been created for.

Idols rob us of the intimacy that God intends to share with us.

God is so good to recapture our hearts and expose the emptiness of idolatry. He will even use the idols in our lives to expose our wrong ways, but only so He can win us back to Himself.

His judgements in our lives are to bring us back to the Presence

---

Lord God, recapture my heart. Thank You for loving me enough to expose the idolatry in my heart so that You might win me back. There is no one like You. I am Yours and You are mine. In Jesus' name, amen.

Dry Bones Live
September 4

Then he said to me, "Prophesy to these bones and say to them, 'Dry bones, hear the word of the Lord! This is what the Sovereign Lord says to these bones: I will make breath enter you, and you will come to life.
Ezekiel 37:4-5

Is there anything more refreshing than getting outside early in the morning to get a deep breath of fresh air?

The last several years, I've learned more about the importance of breath.

When I got into tense situations, I didn't breathe like I was supposed to.

Taking good breaths is essential to stay calm, pump blood throughout your body and have a clear mind when you need to think most.

Breath is even more important than water, food and any other essential need.

If you don't breathe, you don't live for very long.

God's breath being breathed into us is what caused humankind to become living beings.

The breath of God is miraculous.

The breath of God is from the Spirit of God or from the Presence.

In Ezekiel 37, Ezekiel is brought into an encounter with God, where God takes him to a valley full of dry bones. The Lord asks Ezekiel, "Can these bones live?"

The Lord tells him to prophesy, "Dry bones hear the word of the Lord!"

Then the Lord makes His breath enter these dry bones and they begin to rattle, standing up bone to bone until an entire army of dry bones is assembled with flesh and sinew.

Then Ezekiel is told to prophesy to the breath again and the Spirit of God comes upon the bones and causes them to be a living army.

This is a prophetic experience about the nation of Israel, who were like dry bones scattered in judgement. God was saying through this that He would resemble them once again in their land and make them a nation.

Although they were dead as a nation, He was going to bring them back together and cause them to be alive.

This is the power of the Presence.

As Pete Grieg who started 24-7prayer.com used to say, "You see bones, I see an army." *

What if we saw the dead places in our lives, our cities and our society as an opportunity for the breath of God to come and make dry bones live?

What if we saw dire circumstances as an opportunity for God to come and move?

We encounter the Presence through the Word of the Lord and the breath of the Spirit of the Lord.

When we hear God's Word in our lives and let Him breathe upon us, we come alive in His Presence.

He can take any dead thing in our lives, resurrect it and use it for His purpose and glory in us.

Lord, I want to see with Your eyes. Come to the dead and dry places in my life and command them to live. Let dry bones live and become a mighty army. When a people are lost and separate from You, let Your wind blow and bring new life. Let the dead come alive. In Jesus' name, amen.

Another in the Fire
September 5

And these three men, Shadrach, Meshach, and Abed-Nego, fell down bound into the midst of the burning fiery furnace. Then King Nebuchadnezzar was astonished; and he rose in haste and spoke, saying to his counselors, "Did we not cast three men bound into the midst of the fire?" They answered and said to the king, "True, O king." "Look!" he answered, "I see four men loose, walking in the midst of the fire; and they are not hurt, and the form of the fourth is like the Son of God."
Daniel 3:23-25 NKJV

Have you been through a difficult situation that turned out rewarding?

Sometimes we think that our greatest breakthroughs will come when everything is clicking in life and going our way.

My dad often tells me that when he looks back over his life, he realizes that his greatest breakthroughs didn't come when things were easy, but when things were hard.

The tests we enter in life reveal what is really going on in us.

Daniel's three friends, Shadrach, Meshach and Abed-Nego had taken a stand against the demands of Nebuchadnezzar, King of Babylon.

He had a large image of himself made for the people to worship him. He said if anyone did not bow down and worship, they would be thrown in a fiery furnace. Music would play and all the people in the land bowed down to the image of King Nebuchadnezzar, except for Shadrach, Meshach, and Abed-Nego.

The king was furious, so he had the fire stoked seven times hotter and the three of them thrown into the fiery furnace. The fire was so hot it consumed the men who threw them in and it burned off the restraints they were tied up with.

But the fire did not consume these three.

And as they were in the midst of the fire, the king saw one walking as the Son of God. He saw the angel of the Lord or a pre-incarnate Christ, known as a Christophany.

I've heard a preacher say that not bowing down to the idol was the test for Shadrach, Meshach and Abed-Nego, where the fire was the reward for them, because the fire was the place of where Jesus manifested His Presence.

The fires in life can be a time for the Presence. Sometimes it's not until we get into righteous trouble that we realize that Jesus stands with us.

Are you going through a test or a trial?

Are the fires of life burning hot all around you?

Remember, you are not alone. There is another in the fire with you.

The fire is not a punishment, but it's a reward because it's in that place that you will experience His Presence.

His Presence is our greatest reward.

Lord Jesus, You are faithful. You never leave me nor forsake me. You stand with me through every fire and trial in life. There is no one like You. Give me the strength to never compromise and stand with You. You are my reward. I resist complaining when things are tough, knowing this is the place where You manifest Your Presence. In Jesus' name, amen.

Presence Price
September 6

Now when Daniel learned that the decree had been published, he went home to his upstairs room where the windows opened toward Jerusalem. Three times a day he got down on his knees and prayed, giving thanks to his God, just as he had done before.
Daniel 6:10

What would you do if your prayers became illegal?

Christians who lived in certain communist countries know what it is for the practice of their faith to be illegal. Some Christians who live in cultures with a national religion other than the Christian faith know that every time they practice their faith or go to church, they are at risk of going to jail or even worse; they are at risk of death.

It can be hard to imagine in our western culture of America with freedom of religion that we could ever be faced with such a cost for our faith.

However, it is foolish to think in light of human history that the freedoms we enjoy are permanent. The truth is, one day we may have to pay a price for practicing the Presence.

Daniel served not only under King Nebuchadnezzar of Babylon but also under King Darius the Mede after he overthrew Babylon.

The other leaders that Daniel served with under King Darius were trying to plot against him, but the only thing they knew he could be found guilty of was his prayer life.

How would you like to have such a strong prayer life that it's the only reason someone could come after you?

It's kind of like Mary Queen of Scots who said of John Knox, "I fear the prayers of John Knox more than all the assembled armies of Europe."

Daniel knew King Darius had been deceived into signing a law that would send him to the lion's den, but he prayed anyway.

Daniel prayed three times a day and a law against his devotion to the Lord did not change his practice one bit. He got thrown to the lions and the prayers that gave him courage to stand against government orders are the prayers that caused him to be delivered from an overnight stay in a den of lions.

In fact, the very conspirators who plotted against Daniel were the ones who ended up being killed by the lions.

There is a price to pay for the Presence. Sometimes the price is inconvenience or sacrificing sleep. But for some people in the world, devotion to Jesus and practices like prayer can make you guilty of a crime.

Globally, there are many Christians in this generation who are imprisoned, tortured and martyred for their faith. These believers need our prayer and our support. They are heroes who have counted the value and beauty of Jesus as much more worthy than the price they paid. And whatever comes our way, may we count Jesus as worthy of any price that we will have to pay to practice His Presence.

Lord Jesus, You are worthy of my all. No matter what it costs, I choose to seek You in worship and prayer. I ask that You would strengthen the persecuted church with courage and peace as they stand for Your name. May I never take for granted the price that has been paid by the generations before me to practice my faith. In Your holy name, amen.

The People Who Know

September 7

Those who do wickedly against the covenant he shall corrupt with flattery; but the people who know their God shall be strong, and carry out great exploits.
Daniel 11:32 NKJV

What would you say is the key to greatness?

Many people have opinions on what makes someone great.

I've heard my dad say that great men make great decisions.

I think that's true.

But what are the types of decisions that make one great?

I've been privileged to meet many men and women who have done great things in God. I think the key above all other keys is that they knew God.

What does it mean to you to know God?

In our Western culture, to know something is limited to a mental remembrance of facts.

The Biblical Hebrew word for know is "yada." This word for know is about a personal and intimate knowledge of someone.

When Daniel writes of "the people who know their God," he is writing about people who have a firsthand experience of relationship with God.

Daniel elaborates that the people who know their God will be strong and carry out great exploits.

Daniel's life exemplifies this. God raises him up and he does great things because he knows God by practicing the Presence through prayer.

Daniel's prayer life was so powerful it got him arrested and thrown to lions. His prayers were recorded to move angels and demons as he fasted and sought the Lord.

Daniel's prayer life gave him favor with rulers of two of the greatest empires in world history.

Being the people of the Presence is about being the people who know their God.

Knowing God is our greatest calling in this life.

To know Him is to love Him and to live for Him.

If you desire to become strong in your spirit, then seek to know God and treasure knowing Him above all other accomplishments.

God uses those who prize knowing Him above everything else to do great things for Him.

When we care about great things more than knowing Him, we might see Him use us to some measure. But when our greatest desire is knowing Him, then great exploits become the byproduct of a life that abides in the Presence of God and seeks His face out of a love relationship.

Greatness in the Lord comes as we lay down our lives and our striving to know Him and His greatness.

The world doesn't need to be impressed with who we are but needs a people who are impressed with Him.

Lord God, I want to know You. Take me deeper into knowing Your heart. I want to know what You desire and touch Your heart. You are worthy of my whole life. Make me strong and use me to carry out Your purposes. I want to bring You glory. In Jesus' name, amen.

Altars Over Thrones
September 8

Then Elijah said to all the people, "Come here to me." They came to him, and he repaired the altar of the Lord, which had been torn down.
1 Kings 18:30

What do you think is the greatest rivalry of all time?

There are American rivalries like the Hatfields vs. the McCoys. There are sports rivalries like the Lakers vs. Celtics in basketball, the Yankees vs. the Red Sox in baseball, or Alabama vs. Auburn in college football.

The greatest Bible story rivalry is probably David vs. Goliath (besides the overarching battle between God's kingdom and Satan, but that's no contest).

One of the other greatest rivalries in the Bible is Elijah vs. the prophets of Baal.

Elijah had prophesied against Israel and Ahab, the evil king of Israel who was married to the evil queen Jezebel. He prophesied it would not rain in the country until Elijah says that it will rain again.

This is a prophecy against the false god Baal, who supposedly controls the weather.

It doesn't rain for three and a half years.

God uses Elijah to expose the deception of His people's allegiance to this weak idol.

In 1 Kings 18, Elijah invites the 450 prophets of Baal to a challenge. They are both going to build altars and prepare a sacrifice. The God who answers by fire is the one true God.

The prophets of Baal go first and after hours, nothing.

Elijah mocks Baal and the prophets to try harder by being louder and even cutting themselves, but still nothing.

Elijah takes his turn but has a ditch dug around the sacrifice and covers the altar and sacrifice with 12 containers of water. Then he prays and the Lord, who is God.

God answers by fire.

The fire consumes the sacrifice and all the water that had surrounded it.

The people's hearts are turned back to God.

After this Elijah prays and the rain returns to the land. Elijah is a man of the Presence whose prophetic words and prayers stopped and brought back the rain.

Ahab was still the king on the throne in the land, but Elijah rebuilt the altar of the Lord.

He who spends time at the altar has a greater power than he who sits on the throne. The altar is connected to God's throne in heaven. That means the most powerful person on earth is still subject to the most powerful One in heaven.

There is a higher authority than government authority and those who come surrendered before the Presence have greater authority to shift the culture.

People of the Presence realize that true power, authority and greatness are available to those who surrender, sacrifice and yield to the ultimate authority, the Lord God Himself.

There is more available to us in our relationship with God and in prayer than we realize. Stay impressed with the invisible and Almighty Ruler of the universe.

Lord God Almighty, You are the God who answers by fire. Your power exposes the emptiness and weakness of idols and Your enemies. There is no one like You. May I not be impressed with earthy rulers that serve false gods, but may I keep my eyes fixed upon You. In Jesus' name, amen.

Double Portion
September 9

And so it was, when they had crossed over, that Elijah said to Elisha, "Ask! What may I do for you, before I am taken away from you?" Elisha said, "Please let a double portion of your spirit be upon me." So he said, "You have asked a hard thing. Nevertheless, if you see me when I am taken from you, it shall be so for you; but if not, it shall not be so." Then it happened, as they continued on and talked, that suddenly a chariot of fire appeared with horses of fire, and separated the two of them; and Elijah went up by a whirlwind into heaven. And Elisha saw it, and he cried out, "My father, my father, the chariot of Israel and its horsemen!" So he saw him no more. And he took hold of his own clothes and tore them into two pieces.
II Kings 2:9-12 NKJV

Have you ever benefited from someone else ahead of you?

One of the defining moments of my life as a young man was when God called me to follow in my dad's footsteps into the work of the ministry.

I was at a conference in a large church and they asked for everyone to come to the prayer line that night with one specific request.

My friends Todd and Rick asked me what I was going to ask God for in the prayer line that night. I had nothing on my mind.

Rick prophesied, "You are supposed to ask God for the mantle on your dad's life to come upon you."

I doubled over in tears and travail as I felt the call of God stir within me.

Todd added to the word, "It will be a double portion, like from Elijah to Elisha."

I went to tell my dad what happened the next day at his office. I was still so overcome by the Spirit of God I was crying and could barely speak.

My dad's Bible reading plan that morning *just happened* to be on the exact story in 2 Kings 2 of Elijah passing his mantle to Elijah.

My dad prayed for me that day the same prayer as Rick and Todd, for a double portion anointing to be released over my life.

There is an impartation of the Presence that can be released from person to person. If you want to grow deeper in the Presence, the best way to get there besides your own time with God is to spend time with those who are further in than you.

Elijah could impart to Elisha, and Elisha had an increase of anointing because of it.

Don't get me wrong, this is not just about the right timing to rub shoulders with someone, it's about a diligent pursuit and faithful obedience. You can have someone pray for you, but squander what they impart.

Elijah said this was not an easy ask. An impartation for a double portion will send you into a process of trials and tests with power and strength to endure.

Seek the Presence and anointing of the Spirit with all you have.

An impartation will take you further than you can go alone, but it will cost you to steward what you receive.

———

Lord Jesus, I look to You to release a double portion anointing. I want more of You. Let me steward and protect what You deposit in my life. Thank You for others who breakthrough ahead of me and release impartation. In Your name, amen.

Rend Your Heart
September 10

Even now," declares the Lord, "return to me with all your heart, with fasting and weeping and mourning." Rend your heart and not your garments. Return to the Lord your God, for he is gracious and compassionate, slow to anger and abounding in love, and he relents from sending calamity. Who knows? He may turn and relent and leave behind a blessing— grain offerings and drink offerings for the Lord your God.
Joel 2:12-14

Have you ever seen a child give you lip service, but you can tell their heart is not in it?

One thing we look for as parents is to see our children be genuine when they apologize or when they are instructed to do the right thing. Sometimes it's even a little comical to watch a kid try to fake their way through an apology when you can tell their heart isn't in it.

But how rewarding it is as a parent to watch your child put their heart in true repentance and in right actions!

In Joel, God has judged His people Israel with a great army of locusts and a drought that brought destruction to the land. God lets the people know in Joel 2 that He is not looking for an outward form of repentance, He is looking for people to bring Him their heart.

God's judgments are to give people an opportunity to return to Him. His heart relents from sending calamity.

So what is the key to restoring the blessing of the Presence in our lives?

According to this text, it is rending our heart instead of outwardly performing. We are to return, fast and pray, and weep and mourn over our sins.

But again, the key is that our heart is honest before the Lord.

The Lord is not looking for religious ritual and form that is devoid of heartfelt contrition and obedience. God is looking to restore us should we return to Him with all our hearts.

This restoration of God's Presence is revival.

Pastor Mark Brattrud says, "Revival is God's response to our response to His revelation." *

God is longing to revive us when we have turned from Him in our lives, our homes, our churches, and our nations.

Repentance is often looked at as a negative thing because it involves humility as well as confession of our sins and shortcomings.

But repentance restores us and our land so that we can bring our offerings back to God. Our offerings represent His Presence in our lives, the place where God's glory encounters us.

Come before the Lord with a genuine heart of repentance and He will receive you. He is gracious and compassionate, slow to anger and abounding in love.

The Lord will receive you when you return to Him and rend your heart.

Mighty God, I love You! You are gracious and compassionate, slow to anger and abounding in love. You will receive me. Even then, at times I stumble and turn from You. I return to You and rend my heart for my sins, shortcomings, and faults. I mourn over my sins and know that You will bless me as You meet with me. In Jesus' name, amen.

Outpouring of Restoration Rain
September 11

Be glad, people of Zion, rejoice in the Lord your God, for he has given you the autumn rains because he is faithful. He sends you abundant showers, both autumn and spring rains, as before. The threshing floors will be filled with grain; the vats will overflow with new wine and oil. "I will repay you for the years the locusts have eaten— the great locust and the young locust, the other locusts and the locust swarm— my great army that I sent among you.
Joel 2:23-25

Have you ever been in an outpouring?

One time, as a young man, I went alone with my parents to Orlando for vacation. We had finished eating dinner at a large shopping center with a massive parking lot.

The rain started to pour so intensely that it made it impossible to find our car while we stood under a covering. We were looking in the parking lot that was full of rental cars that looked like our rental car.

The heavy rain, thunder, and lightning triggered car alarms, making it hard to locate our vehicle with the key fob. My Dad ran into the parking lot to find the car, but by the time he did, he was soaked through and through; even all the items in his wallet were soaked.

This was a massive outpouring.

God promised Israel a massive outpouring that would restore all that His judgement destroyed and bring about a great harvest supernaturally. He promises an early rain that prepares the harvest and the latter rain that prepares the final harvest before harvest season is over.

When you posture yourself to receive from God, He sends the rain of His Spirit.

When the Presence comes upon us, God releases over us spiritual gifts, restoration, and a harvest of souls.

This is what happened to the church on Pentecost. Peter, under the anointing of the Holy Spirit, got up and used Joel 2 to define what happened when the Spirit was poured out as the church was born.

This is the inheritance for all who receive the Presence:

"And afterward, I will pour out my Spirit on all people. Your sons and daughters will prophesy, your old men will dream dreams, your young men will see visions. Even on my servants, both men and women, I will pour out my Spirit in those days. I will show wonders in the heavens and on the earth, blood and fire and billows of smoke. The sun will be turned to darkness and the moon to blood before the coming of the great and dreadful day of the Lord. And everyone who calls on the name of the Lord will be saved; for on Mount Zion and in Jerusalem there will be deliverance, as the Lord has said, even among the survivors whom the Lord calls." Joel 2:28-32

Holy Spirit, send Your rain. I want to live in the outpouring of the Presence. Fill me with Your spirit and restore all that was lost to me in last seasons. Bring Your abundant rain of restoration to bring a miraculous harvest over my life, my family, my church and my city. In Jesus' name, amen.

FLOW

SEPTEMBER 12

In that day the mountains will drip new wine, and the hills will flow with milk; all the ravines of Judah will run with water. A fountain will flow out of the Lord's house and will water the valley of acacias.
Joel 3:18

Have you ever been in the flow of God's Presence?
It's hard to describe the flow of the Presence in some ways.
In the 1990s, when revival broke out in Toronto, there was a lot of river language used to describe what was happening. I remember singing songs like *Let the River Flow* and *The River is Here* around that time.

I used to think it strange to use language that was so metaphorical and lacked practicality. But when I started to experience the power and Presence of the Holy Spirit with increased measure, I realized why people talked like this.

There is a flow of God's Presence available to everyone through the

Holy Spirit. The river is a glorious place where we experience the glory of God in tangible ways.

In Joel 3, God promises an overflow of abundance where there will be new wine, milk, water and a fountain will overflow from the Lord's house to the valley.

The overflow and outpouring in Joel have to do with the rain, the fountain, and the river of God. The water, the Presence, flows from the Lord's house to this valley.

The valley of acacias is a dry and barren place. Acacias are a light and hard wood that never decay. The Presence never decays.

God is sending His water to the barren and hard to reach places. His flow will bring life and refreshing to people and places that seem resistant.

When you get in the flow of the Spirit, then you become a conduit and source of living water for others. This is the pattern of revival and awakening.

The believer, the family or the church experiences a renewal in the flow of God's Spirit and what works in us can then work through us to touch others.

Be desperate for the flow of God's Presence in your life. It's not only you who will be blessed but everyone that comes in contact with the flow in your life.

I've experienced the Christian life without the flow of the Presence and with the flow. Once I have experienced His nearness and glory in the flow, I never want to go without Him again.

His Presence brings restoration and life to all He touches.

Lord, flow through me! I want to experience the fullness of the new wine, the milk and the water. Let a fountain create a river and flow in me, my family, and my church to touch the dry and dead places around us. I need Your presence. Your Presence is life to me. Let me live in the flow of Your Spirit. In Jesus' name, amen.

Glory Covers
September 13

For the earth will be filled with the knowledge of the glory of the Lord as the waters cover the sea.
Habakkuk 2:14

What is the most recognized brand in the world?

I know that among the most recognized brands are Apple and Coca-Cola. I've been to some pretty remote villages in the jungle of Uganda, and you can find some selling Coca-Cola.

One of the most recognized logos is Nike.

I would imagine that the cross is the most recognized symbol in the world.

The red cross is recognized all around the world as a symbol of humanitarian aid.

I find it interesting to think about what brands, symbols or logos are recognized widely across large groups of people. But what I find most interesting is that millions of people across nations can see something and have a shared knowledge as to what it represents.

The prophet Habakkuk declares that a day is coming where "the earth will be filled with the knowledge of the glory of the Lord as the waters cover the sea."

This is much more, of course, than brand awareness.

Some Bible scholars put this promise at a future date at the return of the Lord, and some see this as representative of a great revival that will sweep the world before Jesus comes back to earth.

We don't have time in this space to discuss the varying views on the millennium and the fullness of God's kingdom being established in the earth. But either way, there is a day coming in the future where the knowledge of the glory, of the Presence, will cover the earth like the waters cover the sea!

God has given us a glimpse now through the Holy Spirit of the greater glory that will sweep the world.

So, the knowledge of God's glory will be filling the earth!

The great longing of humanity is to be reconnected with God. The knowledge of His Presence will sweep all the land, and everyone will understand who He is.

We participate in extending the Presence of God by praying, carrying His Presence, preaching the gospel and making disciples.

God's judgements will be released across the earth in the end, and He will make all things new. He is creating a new heaven and a new earth.

We should marvel at the future hope of the believer. We look forward to this day when He will make all things new, and all the earth will be covered with His glory.

Lord Jesus, as I look forward to Your return, I want to know Your glory and prepare the world for the greater glory that is coming. What a promise You have given, that the knowledge of Your glory will cover the earth like the waters cover the sea! We were made for Your glory and Your Presence. In Your glorious name, amen.

Moses's Tabernacle
September 14

Then the Lord said to Moses, "Come up to the Lord, you and Aaron, Nadab and Abihu, and seventy of the elders of Israel. You are to worship at a distance, but Moses alone is to approach the Lord; the others must not come near. And the people may not come up with him..." When Moses went up on the mountain, the cloud covered it, and the glory of the Lord settled on Mount Sinai. For six days the cloud covered the mountain, and on the seventh day the Lord called to Moses from within the cloud. To the Israelites the glory of the Lord looked like a consuming fire on top of the mountain. Then Moses entered the cloud as he went on up the mountain. And he stayed on the mountain forty days and forty nights.
Exodus 24:1-2, 15-18

What an honor to get an invite into an exclusive meeting. I have been given tickets or invitations to meet people who I really wanted to meet. To get picked and have an opportunity that not everyone receives, bestows such a deep sense of gratitude and appreciation.

Moses received one of the greatest invitations ever. He got invited into the Presence, the place of God's glory that was in a cloud and looked like a consuming fire.

Not everyone received this invitation.

In this invitation, Moses was going to receive the commandments on tablets of stone and then the instructions for the tabernacle. Moses alone got to dwell with God, but he was about to get instructions for the tabernacle, God's sacred tent, so God could come and dwell with His people Israel.

There is so much to learn about the Presence and about God Himself from Moses's tabernacle.

These next several days we will be learning about the tabernacle with help from a great Bible teacher, Ruth Specter Lascelle and her book, *A Dwelling Place for God*. We will learn about God, how the tabernacle points to Jesus Christ, and how we can be His people of the Presence.

"The Sanctuary was prepared by the hands of God Himself and was not only a revelation from Him but also a revelation of Him. Here is where we meet with God face to face and learn to know Him, for in this Tabernacle story He is pictured in His fullness. It is the chief type in all the Scriptures for in it we find the most complete story of redemption. It was a 'shadow' of good things to come, containing the foundation of God's plan for a lost world. Every detail, every bit of material, every color, dimension, position and every article of furniture has its special significance." *

The Bible is a unified story that reveals Jesus to us so that we can know God, the holy Trinity. The tabernacle will show us how to know God more. The more we know Him, the richer the time we have in His Presence.

Lord, I want to learn to dwell with You like Moses and the people of Israel. Teach me from Your tabernacle. There is no like You. I want to live in the glory of Your presence. Thank you for sending Jesus to fulfill all that Moses spoke of that I might draw near as He did. In Jesus' name, amen.

The Offering
September 15

The Lord said to Moses, "Tell the Israelites to bring me an offering. You are to receive the offering for me from everyone whose heart prompts them to give.
Exodus 25:1-2

Have you ever been a part of something with others that you could not do on your own?

I enjoy being a part of a church. It's incredible what can happen when we all do our part to contribute to the community of the church.

Every church does something together that none of us could do alone.

Building a church gives us a place for God to dwell among us and for all of us in the body of Christ to contribute our own unique part that blesses the whole.

The Lord spoke to Moses that there was to be an offering from the heart unto the Lord.

He says their offering goes to Him.

Our giving is an act of worship. Giving is not first to the church but to the Lord.

The giving here was going to build the tabernacle so that the Presence might dwell among them.

We see this today that the giving of our finances, our time and our devotion as the body of Christ creates a dwelling place for Him to rest among us.

Each of the first gifts that God told the Israelites to bring reveal the Lord Jesus in Exodus 25:1-7.

1st Name............ The Lord..................His Title

1st Metal.................Gold................His Divinity

1st Color..........Blue...........His Heavenly Majesty

1st Woven Material....Linen.......His Righteousness

1st Skin...................Ram....................His Will

(Stands Alone)......Acacia Wood........His Humanity

1st Ingredient...........Oil................His Anointing

1st Stone.........Onyx...........His Wisdom and Glory

. . .

Everything that we give should be for Christ Jesus and a reflection of Him. He is worthy.

All of the offerings of our life in the church are to make us a place where Christ is among us.

Our giving and our contribution bring us into the Presence.

"Then have them make a sanctuary for me, and I will dwell among them (Exodus 25:8)."

He has made us His people. When we bring together what He instructs, we make a place for Him to be with us in His manifest Presence.

Lord Jesus, dwell among Your people. Show me where I need to give of my time, my talents and my treasure to contribute to Your body, Your church. May my offerings reflect Christ and may Your church be built up to reflect Christ to the world. Above all, Lord Jesus be glorified. May Your manifest Presence inhabit us so that all might know Your glory. In Your name, amen.

The Ark of The Covenant
September 16

Have them make an ark of acacia wood—two and a half cubits long, a cubit and a half wide, and a cubit and a half high. Overlay it with pure gold, both inside and out, and make a gold molding around it. Cast four gold rings for it and fasten them to its four feet, with two rings on one side and two rings on the other. Then make poles of acacia wood and overlay them with gold. Insert the poles into the rings on the sides of the ark to carry it.
Exodus 25:10-14

Have you ever wondered where the Ark of the Covenant is and what would happen if someone found it?

When I was a boy, I was at a neighbor's house, and I watched *Indiana Jones* and *Raiders of the Lost Ark*.

I wasn't supposed to watch it.

It's a story about a historian/archeologist who goes on adventures to find valuable treasures from history. When the ark was discovered it literally melted people's faces off from the glory of God radiating so strongly from it.

Of course, the real glory of the ark has been now fulfilled in Christ, but I'm still curious as to what it might be like to come near it.

The Ark, this box like furniture, was a place inside the Holy of Holies in the Holy Place or Inner Court of the Tabernacle, which was surrounded by the Outer Court.

Ruth Lascelle, in her book *A Dwelling Place for God,* says, "We see the importance of this piece of furniture in the fact that it is listed first in the directions concerning the building of the Tabernacle. This Ark was to be placed in the Holy of Holies (symbolical of Heaven or God's Throne Room), the innermost room of the Sanctuary where was the Shekinah-Presence. God works from Himself; He moves from Heaven and "comes down"; He proceeds from within, outwards toward man. Man could not go to God if He had not first come to him. The way to God is not of man's invention but of God's revelation. The Tabernacle furniture begins with God's throne. God is first; He will not be second... The Sanctuary of Sinai was to be built that God would dwell 'within.' This is the desire of God for us today - that He be first and the very Center of our lives.'" *

The Ark was revealed by God to be made:

With acacia wood - a hard wood that doesn't rot grew from the desert - a picture of Jesus' humanity who grew in the desert and never rots.

Covered in gold - which speaks of Christ's Divinity.

With a crown - which speaks of Christ's Kingship and authority.

With 4 gold rings - symbolizes endless and eternal love - the Ark was surrounded by God's love. **

The Ark was the container where the Presence came to dwell with us. Jesus is the Ark who came from heaven to us. We don't first seek the Presence in our lives; He came to us first.

———

Lord Jesus, fully human and Divine, thank You that You came from heaven to earth to dwell with us. I worship You. Thank You for the lessons from the Ark. Teach me how to behold Your glory. In Your name, amen.

Inside the Ark

September 17

Then put in the ark the tablets of the covenant law, which I will give you.
Exodus 25:16

Have you ever had a treasure?
What did you do with it?
Did you put it somewhere safe?
I remember watching a television program about home invasion, where some professional security guys broke into a house so they could show a homeowner their vulnerabilities.

It took the pros almost no time to find hidden valuables.

I was shocked because it's the same place I would hide things, and it was not secure.

If we value something, we need to put it somewhere safe.

The ark was a container for something valuable, the law of God. The Ten Commandments that God revealed to Moses were placed inside the Ark. This is a foreshadowing of how the law would be written on the inside in the heart of Jesus and the heart of believers in Jesus (See Ezekiel 36:26).

The Bible also tells us later in Hebrews 9:4 that along with the law, the golden pot of mana and Aaron's rod that budded were also included.

The Ark contained these three items that all revealed Jesus.

Jesus is the Word, as revealed by the law.

Jesus is the Bread of Life as revealed by the mana.

And Jesus is the crucified Savior who brought life through the dead wood of the cross as revealed by the dead rod that miraculously budded to life.

The Ark contained the Word (the law) and it contained the Spirit (the miracles) and it all revealed Jesus.

This was the place the Presence and manifest glory of God rested.

It's all about Jesus.

Those of us who have turned to Jesus through faith encounter the Presence.

Christ dwells in us by faith in the Word and Spirit. His Presence has come to us, and we can abide in His glory.

Lord Jesus, You are the living Word, the Bread of Life and the crucified One who brings life from Your death. There is no one like You. I marvel at Your glory. Thank You for Your Presence. In Your Holy name, amen.

The Mercy Seat
September 18

You shall make a mercy seat of pure gold; two and a half cubits shall be its length and a cubit and a half its width. And you shall make two cherubim of gold; of hammered work you shall make them at the two ends of the mercy seat. Make one cherub at one end, and the other cherub at the other end; you shall make the cherubim at the two ends of it of one piece with the mercy seat. And the cherubim shall stretch out their wings above, covering the mercy seat with their wings, and they shall face one another; the faces of the cherubim shall be toward the mercy seat. You shall put the mercy seat on top of the ark, and in the ark you shall put the Testimony that I will give you. And there I will meet with you, and I will speak with you from above the mercy seat, from between the two cherubim which are on the ark of the Testimony, about everything which I will give you in commandment to the children of Israel.
Exodus 25:17-22 NKJV

Do you have a favorite seat at your house?

My Dad has a reclining chair that's his favorite. We would always try and sit on it with him or take it for ourselves growing up (he got a newer version later on).

Now, my children like to sit with Papa on his reclining chair or snag it for themselves.

Our favorite seat, though, should be the mercy seat.

On top of the Ark of the Covenant sat the mercy seat as described above. We looked at how the contents of the Ark revealed Christ previously, but without the mercy seat, the contents of the law and the mana also served as reminders of Israel's disobedience and grumbling in the desert.

"Without a covering the Ark of the Covenant would have been a judgement throne." *

This is a powerful picture of what James would later say, "Mercy triumphs over judgement (James 2:13)."

The Ark was literally mercy over judgement.

There are many powerful types of Christ and our salvation in the Ark.

The angels were hammered which is a reminder of Christ's suffering.

There were two angels which represented agreement.

We could go on, but ultimately the Ark is a picture of Jesus' death on the cross.

The cross is the place of God's judgment and mercy.

The mercy seat is the place where a lamb's blood was applied once a year by the High Priest on the Day of Atonement.

The New Testament says that Jesus is the Lamb of God and that He is the mercy seat or propitiation.

"And He Himself is the propitiation for our sins, and not for ours only but also for the whole world (I John 2:2 NKJV)."

Jesus is the Lamb slain for us that brings us into God's mercy.

The mercy seat is the place where God meets us with the Presence. It's the place of His glory and where He speaks to us.

All of this is fulfilled in Jesus.

There was no place for a human to sit in the tabernacle, but the mercy seat is the place that God rests and is seated or dwells among His people.

Jesus is said to be a unique High Priest in the book of Hebrews because when He finished His work as High Priest He was seated, unlike the Old Covenant priesthood.

The Presence is a place that we are seated in Christ.

Through His rest, we enter into what He has done to be with Him.

Lord Jesus, You are my mercy seat. I rest in You. Thank You for the cross and defeating the judgement I deserve with mercy. I love You and worship You. Thank You for the blood that cleanses my sin. What a high price that was paid so that I could enter Your Presence by faith. In Your name, amen.

The Table
September 19

Make a table of acacia wood—two cubits long, a cubit wide and a cubit and a half high... Put the bread of the Presence on this table to be before me at all times.
Exodus 25:23, 30

What is your favorite place to be with your family?

My favorite place to be with family is around a table. I love it when we share a delicious meal and have interesting conversations.

A meal around our table is usually loud. My children all try to tell different stories or see who can get a laugh. My wife, Grace, cooks delicious food to fill our stomachs and the time of being together fills our hearts.

This is how I grew up and I enjoy raising our kids the same way, with family dinners around our table several days a week.

The tabernacle had a table set in the holy place or the inner court. It was made of wood and covered in gold. It had many intricacies to its design, but I want to focus on how it represented our fellowship with Christ.

A table is a place for fellowship, and eating a meal together represents the sharing of life with one another.

"To see the face of one," or "to be in his Presence" was considered by the Jews as terms expressive of great favor and honor.

Those who were permitted to see the face of the King were regarded as his favorites and friends.

The bread upon the Golden Table was in the Holy Place in the Presence of the King of glory. What a privilege!

It was also called "Continual Bread."

The King's Table was always abundantly supplied.

Those of us who are redeemed are continually in the Presence of God and are to be communicating with Him as He communicates with us.

His "face" is shining upon us, and our "faces" are ever to shine towards Him. This is holy "communion."" *

This "Bread of the Presence" was ultimately fulfilled in Jesus being the Bread of Life that came down from heaven.

Jesus has connected us to the Presence and because it is through Him, we always have access to this fellowship and communion with God. It's in Jesus that we get to behold the face of God.

Being in the Presence is a place to share our life as He has shared Himself with us.

This is a mutual exchange.

He sets the table for us in giving us Himself, and we keep bread before Him at all times.

He has initiated communion with us, and we respond by communing with Him.

The table is where we meet the Lord in communion.

Lord Jesus, thank You that You gave of Yourself to be the Bread of Life that has come down from heaven. I want to commune with You. As You share Your life with me, I share my life with You. Let me see Your face. I long for a greater fellowship. No one else but You will do. In Your holy name, amen.

The Lampstand
September 20

Make a lampstand of pure gold. Hammer out its base and shaft, and make its flowerlike cups, buds and blossoms of one piece with them.
Exodus 25:31

Were you scared of the dark when you were a child?

I don't know that I feared the dark, but I was scared *in* the dark. I didn't like being in a completely dark room. I always made sure my parents left the door cracked at night and the hallway light on so I could have some light in my room. Of course, God made the night and the dark so we could have a time of rest we certainly need (which I would learn later in life), but it's good to love the light.

In the Inner Court, or Holy Place of the Tabernacle, was the Lampstand with 7 lights. This was not a lampstand with 7 wax candles, rather it was a single hammered piece of gold that had 7 lights and that were fueled by oil. The Holy Place was covered and the only light inside was the light from the Lampstand.

God did not give specific measurements for this like He did other pieces of the Tabernacle.

"He does not give any measurement to it. God has as much purpose in omitting instructions as He does including them in His Word. There is no measure or dimensions given for this Lampstand; there is no measure to light! Light is limitless, without dimension; so the Lord Jesus in His measure of light, love, truth, grace and mercy is matchless and limitless." *

Jesus is the light of the Tabernacle and the whole world.

"When Jesus spoke again to the people, he said, 'I am the light of the world. Whoever follows me will never walk in darkness, but will have the light of life.'" (John 8:12 NIV).

It is by Jesus that we see God and that we see all of life. When we see and know Jesus, the rest of our life comes into focus. When we are in the Presence and so close to our Lord, our eyes see so clearly in His light.

It is so important to come near Him so He can show us where we need to repent, where we need His encouragement, or where we could be living under lies. Through faith in Jesus, we get to come near the Presence daily and He is still illuminating our lives as the light.

Remember, the glory of God shines in the face of Jesus (See 2 Corinthians 4:6).

Lord Jesus, I run to You, Light of the world and Light of my life. Search me. Reveal Your truth to me, about me and about all that You need me to see in this hour. You are the matchless and limited One. In Your light, there is hope, healing and freedom. I love You! In Your precious name, amen.

The Veil
September 21

You shall make a veil woven of blue, purple, and scarlet thread, and fine woven linen. It shall be woven with an artistic design of cherubim.
Exodus 26:31 NKJV

Have you ever seen a child get a gift so big it can't be wrapped?

As a child, when a gift was too big to be wrapped conventionally, it usually meant a great gift. Something like a blanket or curtain had to be used to cover a wagon, a bicycle or a basketball hoop.

Whenever a gift was covered by something large to hide it, I would get so excited to see what was behind it.

Between the Most Holy Place, the Holy of Holies and the Inner Court was a veil.

The first mention of a door or gate between entries in the Tabernacle is the veil, which is the innermost entry. The Tabernacle is always heaven to earth. The Presence is always moving from heaven to earth.

This veil was set up to separate these two rooms where the High

Priest could only enter once a year behind the veil in the Holy of Holies. The veil was concealing the greatest glory and gift where the Ark rested, the manifest Presence of God Almighty.

This veil protected the great gift of God's glory and also protected the priests who ministered to the Lord in the Inner Court from the raw power of God they could not handle approaching regularly. The veil was beautiful and had much depth to its symbolism, but it also served this important function which showed extreme honor for the manifest Presence of God.

When Jesus died on the cross, the veil of the temple was torn in two from top to bottom. It was ripped from heaven to earth (See Matthew 27:51-52).

The writer of Hebrews would later go on to give deeper meaning to what happened on the cross. "Therefore, brethren, having boldness to enter the Holiest by the blood of Jesus, by a new and living way which He consecrated for us, through the veil, that is, His flesh." (Hebrews 10:19-20 NKJV).

Not only did Jesus' death cause the veil to be torn, His body became the veil for us somehow on the cross that opened up the way for us to enter the Most Holy Place by His blood.

Jesus' death tore the veil for us and He was the veil torn for us. You have boldness to enter into His Presence.

The place where priests feared to tread and was concealed by the veil is open to you and I. We often don't realize what a holy price was paid for us to be granted such easy access into the Presence.

Don't take for granted what He has done. It wasn't a cheap price, it cost Him everything.

The price paid for us gives us the confidence to access this now. Enter in beloved child of God to the place purchased for you through the body of Christ.

Lord Jesus, You became the veil torn for me to enter the Most Holy Place by Your blood. I refuse to stay in the Outer and Inner Court when You have made the way for me to come boldly to the place Your glory dwells. I thank You and worship You for the great price You paid to open the way from heaven to earth. In Your holy name, amen.

The Altar
September 22

Build an altar of acacia wood, three cubits high; it is to be square, five cubits long and five cubits wide.
Exodus 27:1

What is your favorite number?

I don't believe in lucky numbers and I think sometimes Christians get too interested in numbers and treat them like they are lucky. But it's also foolish to ignore the important emphasis God puts on numbers in the Scripture.

My favorite number is five.

Why?

Because it's my wife's favorite number.

Her name is Grace and five is known Biblically speaking as the number of grace. The tabernacle points us to Jesus, and the number 5 is a part of what points to Him.

The altar was a place for sacrifices offered to the Lord.

The altar is a picture for us of the cross where Jesus was the ultimate sacrifice.

The altar was five cubits square. Here is a big part of how fiverepresents grace:

"This "slaughter place" was to be five cubits square--five all the way around. It is interesting to note, in this connection, that there were not only FIVE wounds? but FIVE KINDS of wounds given to Christ on when God's grace to man was manifested on Golgotha's Altar. He suffered every type of flesh wound known to medical science!

Five bleeding wounds He bears, Received on Calvary, They pour effectual prayers, They strongly plead for me. "Forgive him, O forgive' they cry, 'Nor let that ransomed sinner die! Nor let that ransomed sinner die!'" *

"Emphasis was placed on plainness so that the altar itself should not become the object of veneration or worship. God's instructions to His people Israel excluded metal and hewn stone in the offering place because this would involve man's ability. (Being hollow, the Altar man built could not have anything man-made in its center)! God wants an altar that He Himself has planned and fashioned." **

The Lord has prepared the altar for us to meet with Him and come into the Presence. He has made the way for us by the cross. His wounds are His grace for us and for our healing (See Isaiah 53).

We don't earn the Presence. He gives us Himself by His grace.

Lord Jesus, I come to Your altar, the cross. You meet me at Your cross. I receive Your grace. You were wounded for my healing. There is no one like You. In Your perfect name, amen.

The Sacrifice
September 23

Make the altar hollow, out of boards. It is to be made just as you were shown on the mountain.
Exodus 27:8

Have you ever thought about what it would be like to be part of a family who brought a sacrifice to the tabernacle of Moses?

It must have been incredible to see thousands of Israelite families bringing their sin offerings to the Tabernacle. The priests slaughtered hundreds and thousands of animals in a single day.

Could you imagine an animal you raised or purchased being gathered up by your dad to drag to God's sacred tent for a sacrifice for your sins?

"The Hebrew word for altar is "mizbeah," meaning "slaughter place." And truly it was a symbol of suffering, blood-shed, and death. The only approach to a holy God in His Tabernacle was by way of this object of wood and copper. The altar would have been of no avail without the offerings which were presented to God upon it. No Israelite could approach it without the sacrifices and the blood. "Without shedding of blood is no remission."" *

"What significance does it have for us to-day? Here we see God's goodness and severity, HIS Love and wrath, His righteousness and peace. It is here that the heart of man and the heart of God are revealed, and atonement for sin is made. At this altar the innocent bore the judgment of the guilty, and God was reconciled with the sinner Who killed and shed the blood of the sacrifice. This "slaughter place" pictures the cross of Calvary, a vessel on earth which is the only way of entrance into God's Presence. It depicts the Cross which is easily accessible to the world but towers over all the wrecks of time, the cross upon which the Prince of Glory died, where He was bound with the cords of love for lost humanity." **

God gave specific instructions in Leviticus 1-8 for the types of offerings that were to be brought to the altar for the people of Israel that were fulfilled on the cross:

BURNT OFFERING..........CONSECRATION

MEAL OFFERING............SERVICE

PEACE OFFERING...........FELLOWSHIP

SIN OFFERING................REDEMPTION (for the sinner)

TRESPASS OFFERING......REDEMPTION (for sin) ***

Jesus was the sacrifice that ended all sacrifices on the altar of the cross. His blood sacrifice paid for all our sin once and for all. We now have perpetual access to the Presence through the acceptable offering of Jesus the Lamb of God (See Hebrews 9-10).

Lord Jesus, You are the ultimate sacrifice for my sin. Your offering has brought me into consecration, service, fellowship and redemption. I have peace with You and entrance into Your glorious Presence. In Your worthy name, amen.

Deeper

September 24

For the gate of the court there shall be a screen twenty cubits long, woven of blue, purple, and scarlet thread, and fine woven linen, made by a weaver. It shall have four pillars and four sockets.
Exodus 27:16 NKJV

Were you ever amazed by how much bigger the inside of a building was than you'd imagined?

The church we pastor meets in a warehouse and I often hear from people who are newer that they are surprised by everything that fits inside.

There are so many rooms, hallways and doors, people get kind of lost inside sometimes. The deeper you go, there is more to see.

While the warehouse may not look like much from the outside, it is full of amazing people who are hungry for God in the center where we worship Jesus in the sanctuary.

The deeper you go in the building, you realize there is more for you to experience and see.

Every part and detail of the Tabernacle had significant meaning. The Tabernacle had three curtains called the veil, the door and the gate.

The veil separated the Holy of Holies from the Holy Place (or Inner Court). The door separated the Inner Court from the Outer Court. Finally, the Gate separated the Outer Court from the camp outside and was the entrance into the Tabernacle.

Jesus is the entrance through the gate, the door, and the veil. This imagery is throughout the Psalms, John and Hebrews.

The way to go deeper into the Presence is always through Jesus. Many people in American Christianity seem to think Jesus is where you start, but then you have to move on to go deeper. There is nothing deeper than Jesus, the incarnate God who came to us making a way from heaven to earth through His perfect offering on the cross.

I often say there is not more than the gospel, but there is more *in* the gospel. All depth is truly found in Jesus, yet as the tabernacle shows us, we may have entered into the gate, but there is so much more for us deeper behind the door and the veil.

This doesn't mean there are specific levels of superiority. But it does show that we must respond with hunger and willingness to grow in our relationship with God through Jesus.

Many Christians are content to stay back in the comfort of the outer court.

Jesus had about 500 somewhat faithful followers after His death and resurrection, but only 120 waited on Him in the upper room.

Jesus had 70 disciples in Luke 10. But He spent most of His time with 12.

Of the 12, only 3 were intimately close and only 1 was truly there for Him in His greatest time of need.

Jesus appeared to 500, but why did only 120 press into the promise?

Jesus chose 12, but why did only 3 stay close?

The answer is they went deeper into relationship with Him.

Don't be content, believer, to stay in the outer court.

Go deeper in Him.

It's all about Jesus, but there is more in Him than you know or have experienced. The deeper you go, the greater the glory and the more of His Presence is available.

May You take the invitation to go deeper and closer to His heart.

———

Lord Jesus, all of my life is found in You. Call me past the Outer Courts and into the Holy Place. Take me deeper still behind the Veil into the Most Holy Place. I want to know Your heart and continue on this journey of pressing into greater glory! O that I might behold the glory of Your dwelling place. In Your Holy name, amen.

Atonement Day
September 25

And Aaron shall make atonement upon its horns once a year with the blood of the sin offering of atonement; once a year he shall make atonement upon it throughout your generations. It is most holy to the Lord.
Exodus 30:10 NKJV

Do you know what the day of atonement is?

The Day of Atonement or Yom Kippur is the most solemn day of all Jewish Holidays.

Yom Kippur is the day referred to in Exodus 30, where the high priest goes into the Most Holy Place once a year to apply the blood of the sin offering.

There were sacrifices made all throughout the year for sin, but only on the Day of Atonement could the High Priest go behind and the Veil to atone for his own sins and the sins of all of Israel before the Ark of the Covenant. This day is commemorated by Jews with a 26 hour fast with contemplation and prayer over their sins. *

In the book of Hebrews, we learn that the Tabernacle of Moses was actually created after the Tabernacle in heaven.

Moses's Tabernacle, as great as it was, was actually a copy of what is in heaven. I realize we have been covering what the Ark, the Mercy Seat and the sacrifices represented as they all pointed to Jesus. But I want you to see from the Scripture itself that the Day of Atonement was a picture of what Jesus did after He died on the cross; not once a year, but once for all by making the way for us eternally into the Presence, where He applied His blood for us in heaven.

"Now when these things had been thus prepared, the priests always went into the first part of the tabernacle, performing the services. But into the second part the high priest went alone once a year, not without blood, which he offered for himself and for the people's sins committed in ignorance; the Holy Spirit indicating this, that the way into the Holiest of All was not yet made manifest while the first tabernacle was still standing. It was symbolic for the present time in which both gifts and sacrifices are offered which cannot make him who performed the service perfect in regard to the conscience— concerned only with foods and drinks, various washings, and fleshly ordinances imposed until the time of reformation. But Christ came as High Priest of the good things to come, with the greater and more perfect tabernacle not made with hands, that is, not of this creation. Not with the blood of goats and calves, but with His own blood He entered the Most Holy Place once for all, having obtained eternal redemption. For if the blood of bulls and goats and the ashes of a heifer, sprinkling the unclean, sanctifies for the purifying of the flesh, how much more shall the blood of Christ, who through the eternal Spirit offered Himself without spot to God, cleanse your conscience from dead works to serve the living God? And for this reason He is the Mediator of the new covenant, by means of death, for the redemption of the transgressions under the first covenant, that those who are called may receive the promise of the eternal inheritance." Hebrews 9:6-15 NKJV

As of this writing, today September 25, 2023, is the Day of Atonement or Yom Kippur until the evening (as a Jewish day is from evening to evening). This is a good time to meditate on what Christ has done to pay for your sins and make atonement for you to receive your eternal inheritance.

This is a good day to turn from sin and live in the fullness of what Jesus paid for by applying His own blood for you in the Holy of Holies.

Lord Jesus, You are the Sacrifice and the High Priest. Your blood has atoned for my sin and given me an eternal inheritance. Search my heart and grant me repentance. Cleanse me and renew me. Let me live in holiness and purity by the power of Your blood and the access I now have eternally to Your Presence. In Your name, amen.

THE BURNING LAMP
SEPTEMBER 26

And you shall command the children of Israel that they bring you pure oil of pressed olives for the light, to cause the lamp to burn continually.
Exodus 27:20 NKJV

Do you think that it's more important in your spiritual life to have large, life-changing events or small daily steps of faithfulness?

In my life, I've had incredible encounters with God that are defining moments.

When I got delivered from oppression and freed from life controlling sinful habits, it was a chapter marker in my life.

When I got called to ministry prophetically, my life was never the same.

When I received prayer from Leif Hetland and Randy Clark, I received an impartation of love and power from the Holy Spirit that has changed me forever.

But one thing I have learned is that when I don't take small daily steps of faithful obedience to spend time with Jesus in prayer and His Word, the vibrancy of my spiritual life wanes.

We need both dramatic events with God, but also consistent daily steps of obedience to continually grow in God.

The Tabernacle was the very Dwelling Place for God. It was an incredible and glorious Tent for the manifest glory of God to reside. Things don't get more powerful and dramatic than the glory of God that rested in the midst of the Tabernacle.

But this reality of God dwelling among His people was sustained by the daily obedience of the Levites; the Priests and the people of Israel faithfully carrying out their duties.

The Israelites were to supply fresh olive oil for the burning of the lamp.

In our Christian life, God ignites a fire in us through the Holy Spirit, but we need to keep fueling the lamp and fanning the flame. It's not up to our works and self-efforts to grow in God, but when God initiates something in our life, He looks for our response and participation in what He is doing.

In Ephesians five we are instructed to "be filled with the Holy Spirit."

Which of course, is only possible with God filling us, but the instruction is to us, which shows that we affect whether we actually are being filled.

This is the picture we see of the Israelites supplying fresh oil for the lamp.

We need to have a daily relationship with God to sustain our growth in the Presence. We need to continue to feed the work of God in our lives. You can't live on yesterday's oil; you need a fresh encounter with God.

All relationships that quit being nurtured end up drifting apart.

Don't let the fire of first love burn out in your life. Keep feeding that fire with fresh oil.

Jesus, touch my heart afresh with Your holy fire. Fill me with Your Holy Spirit. Help me nurture and invest in my spiritual growth daily. Give me a greater hunger for Your Presence and for Your Word. I want a fresh touch every day. In Your worthy name, amen.

The Preisthood
September 27

Now take Aaron your brother, and his sons with him, from among the children of Israel, that he may minister to Me as priest, Aaron and Aaron's sons: Nadab, Abihu, Eleazar, and Ithamar. And you shall make holy garments for Aaron your brother, for glory and for beauty. So you shall speak to all who are gifted artisans, whom I have filled with the spirit of wisdom, that they may make Aaron's garments, to consecrate him, that he may minister to Me as priest.
Exodus 28:1-3 NKJV

Have you seen yourself as a priest?

I remember being in an Eastern country and seeing people worshiping the idols they had created. They prayed prayers, sang songs and cooked food for their gods. One person even hired a DJ to play music for their god into the early hours of the morning outside the building I slept in, which definitely affected my sleep.

Idolatry is wrong and condemned in the Bible as one of the sins that God detests the most.

But I thought it was interesting to see how these people saw themselves as a priest more clearly than some Christians see themselves.

A priest is called by God to first minister to the Lord.

God chose Aaron that "He may minister to Me (the Lord) as priest."

A Christian's first ministry and calling is not to people but to minister to the Lord Himself.

We don't first minister for the Lord but *to* Him.

Jesus is the great High Priest (See Hebrews 7-9).

He is the fulfillment of every part of the Tabernacle, but in Him, we share in His ministry.

Jesus is the Son of God who makes us children of God.

Jesus is the light of the world who makes the church the light of the world.

Jesus is the great Reconciler who gives us the ministry of reconciliation.

Jesus shares His ministry of being a Priest with us.

"You also, as living stones, are being built up a spiritual house, a holy priesthood, to offer up spiritual sacrifices acceptable to God through Jesus Christ" (I Peter 2:5 NKJV).

"And they sang a new song, saying: "You are worthy to take the scroll, And to open its seals; For You were slain, And have redeemed us to God by Your blood Out of every tribe and tongue and people and nation, And have made us kings and priests to our God; And we shall reign on the earth" (Revelation 5:9-10 NKJV).

When we worship God and pray to Him, we are living out our role as priests.

When we attend to His will, His desire and His heart first, we are fulfilling our calling as priests.

Attending church is not first about ministering to others or even about hearing sermons where others minister to us.

Have you ever thought, "What is the point of going to church if I just sing songs and hear someone else talk about God?"

The point is first to come together with all other believers who are in this royal priesthood to bring spiritual sacrifices to God that minster to His heart.

He is worthy of our ministry as priests.

Father God, thank You for Jesus, my great High Priest. Thank You for sharing the ministry of a priest with me in Christ. Teach me to minister to Your heart. I want to touch Your heart and bring spiritual sacrifices of praise that bless, honor, and glorify You. In the wonderful name of Jesus, amen.

Consecration
September 28

Then you shall kill the ram, and take some of its blood and put it on the tip of the right ear of Aaron and on the tip of the right ear of his sons, on the thumb of their right hand and on the big toe of their right foot, and sprinkle the blood all around on the altar. And you shall take some of the blood that is on the altar, and some of the anointing oil, and sprinkle it on Aaron and on his garments, on his sons and on the garments of his sons with him; and he and his garments shall be hallowed, and his sons and his sons' garments with him.
Exodus 29:20-21 NKJV

Do you have something in your home that is set apart for special days?

When I was growing up, my mom had a special plate she put out for our birthdays. It was set apart for whoever was the birthday boy or birthday girl.

In fact, the plate said "You are special today" and it was bright red. Getting the red plate meant I was first in line for my special birthday meal, which was always important to me and actually did make me feel special.

As priests, Aaron and his sons were not only to wear the right garments, they were to be consecrated or set apart for their service. The priestly garments had deep and beautiful meaning. They were anointed with oil and prepared in several steps to be ready for service.

I want to draw attention to the part of the consecration that had to do with the application of blood. The priests were to have the blood of a lamb (the ram) applied to their right ear, their right thumb and their right big toe.

A priest needed blood applied to them to be ready for holy service.

The blood applied to the ear represents the need for a priest to be consecrated to hear the voice of God. The blood applied to the right thumb represents the need for a priest to have his ministry work consecrated. And the blood applied to the right big toe represents the need for the priest to have his walk with God consecrated.

This is true for the believer as a priest in the New Covenant, as well. We need the blood of Jesus to set us apart in our relationship with God (our hearing His voice). We need the blood of Jesus to set us apart in our ministry to God and others (the work of our hands). And we need the blood of Jesus to set us apart in our lifestyle (the walk with our feet).

The blood of Jesus is applied not only to our souls to save us from our sin but also to consecrate for life and ministry in the Presence.

Let us apply the power of the blood of Jesus to our hearing, our hands, and our feet. May God cleanse our motives, our efforts and our steps to bring glory and honor to Him.

Pray these song lyrics today: *

Glory to His name

. . .

Glory to His name

There to my heart was the blood applied

Glory to His name

Amen.

Incense

September 29

You shall make an altar to burn incense on; you shall make it of acacia wood. And you shall put it before the veil that is before the ark of the Testimony, before the mercy seat that is over the Testimony, where I will meet with you. "Aaron shall burn on it sweet incense every morning; when he tends the lamps, he shall burn incense on it. And when Aaron lights the lamps at twilight, he shall burn incense on it, a perpetual incense before the Lord throughout your generations.
Exodus 30:1, 6-8 NKJV

What is your favorite aroma?

I think my favorite smells are my wife's perfume and the wonderful baking she does. She makes our house smell great by keeping everything clean, lighting candles and did I already mention the wonderful smells of her baking?

A smell has the power to bring you back to certain memories, change the atmosphere, and bring you joy.

The altar of incense was a part of the tabernacle, and it was to be offered to the Lord perpetually as a beautiful smelling aroma. The tabernacle was a full sensory experience for the worshippers in the place that God's glory dwelt.

The book of Revelation gives us some insights into what the incense offered before the Lord represents:

"Now when He had taken the scroll, the four living creatures and the twenty-four elders fell down before the Lamb, each having a harp, and golden bowls full of incense, which are the prayers of the saints" (Revelation 5:8 NKJV).

"Then another angel, having a golden censer, came and stood at the altar. He was given much incense, that he should offer it with the prayers of all the saints upon the golden altar which was before the throne. And the smoke of the incense, with the prayers of the saints, ascended before God from the angel's hand. Then the angel took the censer, filled it with fire from the altar, and threw it to the earth. And there were noises, thunderings, lightnings, and an earthquake" (Revelation 8:3-5 NKJV).

The incense offered to the Lord was a symbol of prayers that are to rise to the Lord in the Presence around the clock. The Book of Revelation says God keeps believers' prayers in bowls.

These prayers are not only stored, they are released back to the earth in a major way. Our prayers, when answered, are likened to thunder, lightning, and earthquakes.

Our time ministering to the Lord in our prayers rises as incense but then is released back to the earth in power.

Lord Jesus, You are worthy of perpetual prayer and worship. You are worthy of prayers that touch Your heart day and night. Let my prayers and the prayers of Your people rise as incense to Your throne. Show us the power of our prayers that You store in Your heavenly bowls and release the answers back into the earth. In Your powerful name, amen.

WASH
SEPTEMBER 30

Then the Lord spoke to Moses, saying: "You shall also make a laver of bronze, with its base also of bronze, for washing. You shall put it between the tabernacle of meeting and the altar. And you shall put water in it, for Aaron and his sons shall wash their hands and their feet in water from it. When they go into the tabernacle of meeting, or when they come near the altar to minister, to burn an offering made by fire to the Lord, they shall wash with water, lest they die. So they shall wash their hands and their feet, lest they die. And it shall be a statute forever to them—to him and his descendants throughout their generations.
Exodus 30:17-21 NKJV

Did your mom always make you wash up before dinner?

My wife is always making sure our kids have clean hands. She gets them to wash regularly, or she passes out hand sanitizer.

Sometimes I think it's the extreme end, but it is actually a good habit. I'm thankful she keeps them clean.

The tabernacle furnishings include the laver or a washbasin for the priest to wash their hands. The priests needed to wash their hands and feet to minister to the Lord.

Nothing unclean could withstand the intensity of God's glory and one could die without washing their hands and feet. Those giving an offering to the Lord and ministering in the tabernacle were not only properly clothed and consecrated but also needed to be clean.

Having clean hands spiritually is a pre-requisite to enter the Presence.

"Who may ascend into the hill of the Lord? Or who may stand in His holy place? He who has clean hands and a pure heart, Who has not lifted up his soul to an idol, Nor sworn deceitfully" (Psalms 24:3-4 NKJV).

David knew that to enter the holy place, you needed to have clean hands, which he connected to a pure heart.

O saint, I have good news for you!

We as believers in Jesus receive the washing we need to be clean before His Presence by Him!

In Ephesians, when Paul is instructing the church about marriage, he likens Jesus to a groom that cares for His bride, the church.

He says, "that He (Jesus) might sanctify and cleanse her (the church) with the washing of water by the word" (Ephesians 5:26 NKJV).

Jesus is the perfect husband who washes and cleanses His bride with His Word.

Coming into the Presence is always coming through Jesus. How do we come through Jesus? By the Spirit and the Word. It is so important to spend time in the Scripture to cleanse our hands and our feet, so to speak.

The Word washes us and cleanses us and ushers us into the holy place.

Jesus, thank You for Your Holy Word. Let Your Word wash over me. Wash me and I will be clean. Wash me and renew me. Your Word ushers me into Your Presence. It's through Your Word that I know You, Jesus, and even know who I am. Wash me to be fit for Your Presence. In Your holy name, amen.

Bibliography

July 7th
The Westminster Shorter Catechism. Westminster Assembly, 1647.
July 24th
The NIV Study Bible. Edited by Kenneth L. Barker, Full rev. ed., Zondervan, 2011.
August 10th
Tozer, A. W. *The Pursuit of God.* Moody Publishers, 1948.
August 12th
Bishop Jospeh Garlington https://www.bishopjlg.com/
August 16th
Graham Cook https://brilliantperspectives.com/
August 26th
The opportunity of a lifetime must be seized during the lifetime of the opportunity.— attributed to Leonard Ravenhill
August 30th
Ravenhill, Leonard. *Why Revival Tarries.* Bethany House Publishers, 1959.
September 4th
https://www.24-7prayer.com/
September 10th
https://www.youtube.com/live/WYIzwCpMf20?si=IJO5qh9Ch3GbWqzs
September 14th
Lascelle, Ruth Specter; *A Dwelling Place for God,* p. 1.
September 16th
Lascelle, Ruth Specter; *A Dwelling Place for God,* p. 25-26.
**Lascelle, summaries from p. 26-30.
September 18th
Lascelle, Ruth Specter; *A Dwelling Place for God,* p. 37.
September 19th
Lascelle, Ruth Specter; *A Dwelling Place for God,* p. 53-54.
September 20th
Lascelle, Ruth Specter; *A Dwelling Place for God,* p. 61.
September 22nd
* Lascelle, Ruth Specter; A Dwelling Place for God, & Arise my Soul Arise by Charles Wesley p. 124-125
**Lascelle, Ruth Specter; A Dwelling Place for God, p. 134
September 23rd
*Lascelle, Ruth Specter; *A Dwelling Place for God,* p. 139
**Lascelle, Ruth Specter; *A Dwelling Place for God,* p. 141
***Lascelle, Ruth Specter; *A Dwelling Place for God,* p. 140
September 25th

https://www.chabad.org/library/article_cdo/aid/177886/jewish/What-Is-Yom-Kippur.htm

September 28th
The hymn "Glory to His Name," also known as "Down at the Cross," written by Elisha A. Hoffman in 1878 and with music by John H. Stockton. Public domain.

BOOKS BY JOHN HAMMER

eXXXit

The Presence Series:

- The Lord of the Presence
- The Power of the Presence
- The Pursuit of the Presence
- The Wonder of the Presence

Altars over Thrones (forthcoming)

Contact

To continue to get more writing and updates from John or invite John to speak go subscribe to his Substack at johnandhammer.substack.com

About the Author

John Hammer is married to the love of his life Grace Elaine and Dad to four amazing children: Hailey, Emma, Justus and Addison. John is a graduate of Seattle Bible College. He loves communication through preaching, teaching, writing poetry and prose, as well as theological or philosophical conversations. He enjoys laughter at family dinners and staying active with them through Brazilian-Jiu Jitsu, Pickleball, and river walks. He and Grace are the Lead Pastors at Sonrise Christian Center in Everett, WA. He is also a co-founder of The Way and Represent Conferences. Johnandhammer.substack.com | isonrise.org

www.ingramcontent.com/pod-product-compliance
Lightning Source LLC
Chambersburg PA
CBHW020923090426

42736CB00010B/1022